SKY BELOW

SKY

A BILINGUAL EDITION

RAÚL ZURITA

BELOW

SELECTED WORKS

TRANSLATED FROM THE SPANISH AND WITH
AN INTRODUCTION BY ANNA DEENY MORALES

 Curbstone Books | Northwestern University Press | Evanston, Illinois

Curbstone Books
Northwestern University Press
www.nupress.northwestern.edu

Printed in the United States of America

10 9 8 7 6 5 4 3 2 1

ISBN 978-0-8101-3384-6 (paper)

Library of Congress Cataloging-in-Publication Data are available from the Library of Congress.

The paper used in this publication meets the minimum requirements of the American National Standard for Information Sciences—Permanence of Paper for Printed Library Materials, ANSI Z39.48–1992.

CONTENTS

Acknowledgments   vii

Zurita: On the Disappeared and Beloved   ix
Anna Deeny Morales

De *PURGATORIO* | From *PURGATORY*

EN EL MEDIO DEL CAMINO | IN THE MIDDLE OF
THE ROAD   6

DESIERTOS | DESERTS   16

ÁREAS VERDES | GREEN AREAS   30

MI AMOR DE DIOS | MY LOVE OF GOD   38

LA VIDA NUEVA | NEW LIFE   46

De *ANTEPARAÍSO* | From *ANTEPARADISE*

LAS UTOPÍAS | UTOPIAS   60

CORDILLERAS | CORDILLERAS   68

PASTORAL | PASTORAL   76

*CANTO A SU AMOR DESAPARECIDO | SONG FOR HIS
DISAPPEARED LOVE*   92

De *LA VIDA NUEVA* | from *NEW LIFE*

LA VIDA NUEVA | NEW LIFE   132

I. LOS RÍOS ARROJADOS | THE RIVERS CAST DOWN   136

II. LAS BORRADAS ESTRELLAS | THE STARS ERASED   148

III. LOS RÍOS DEL CIELO | THE RIVERS OF SKY   152

De *POEMAS MILITANTES* | From *MILITANT POEMS*   160

De *INRI* | From *INRI*

EL MAR | THE SEA   168

BRUNO SE DOBLA, CAE | BRUNO BENDS OVER, FALLS   176

De *ZURITA* | From *ZURITA*

TU ROTA TARDE | YOUR BROKEN AFTERNOON   194

TU ROTA NOCHE | YOUR BROKEN NIGHT   216

TU ROTO AMANECER | YOUR BROKEN DAWN   226

Works by Raúl Zurita   259

List of Poems   261

Illustration Credits   267

ACKNOWLEDGMENTS

The author and translator thank Forrest Gander, Paulina Wendt, Valerie Mejer, Francine Masiello, and Sharmistha Mohanty for their friendship, attentive readings of the manuscript, and unwavering love for poetry. We also thank our families.

> Do not . . . make me sit on a chair while Hektor
> lies yet forlorn among the shelters; rather with all speed
> give him back, so my eyes may behold him . . .
> —Homer, *Iliad*

> For years, the silent landscapes of Chile—its volcanoes
> and mountains, its desert and ocean, its lakes and
> rivers—were the only ones to receive those remains.
> Theirs was the only mercy that welcomed those bodies
> destroyed by an aberrant order that didn't even fulfill
> its ancestral and archaic gesture anchored in what is
> profoundly human: to return to families the cadavers
> of their fallen kin.
> —Raúl Zurita, "From the Memory and Dream"

Raúl Zurita often speaks of the *Iliad's* last book, in which Priam, the Trojan king, travels into the enemy Acheaen camp desperate to behold and retrieve the corpse of his son, Hektor. Priam eventually recovers his son, whose many wounds from defilement and decay are erased thanks to Apollo's divine intervention. The *Iliad's* final scene depicts Hektor's magnificent obsequies, as the Acheaens have granted the Trojans twelve days of peace so they may properly mourn their kinsman before the definitive razing of their city. This story reflects what Zurita and many others consider the most egregious abuses of General Augusto Pinochet's military regime, namely, the desecration and "disappearance" of thousands of individuals whose remains were never returned to their loved ones. With the help of the CIA and U.S. military forces, Pinochet overthrew the democratically elected government led by Salvador Allende during a multifront coup d'état on September 11, 1973.[1] Allende's socialist platform included a national healthcare program; the distribution of milk to infants, children, and pregnant women; educational and agrarian reform; as well as the nationalization of the country's banks and copper industry. Throughout the coup and the ensuing seventeen-year dictatorship, anyone suspected of opposing the fascist state's enforcement of capitalism and its concomitant values risked arrest, imprisonment, torture, and disappearance.[2] Zurita was among those rounded up at dawn on September 11 in Valparaiso, where he was a university student studying engineering. He was detained for several months along with hundreds of other prisoners in the hold of a ship called the *Maipo* docked at the city's port.

The 1991 *Report of the Chilean National Commission for Truth and Reconciliation*, known as the Rettig Report, identified the disappearance of bodies as the first in a list of human rights abuses committed by Pinochet's government.[3] Through "death flights," soldiers pushed prisoners over the "silent landscapes of Chile," into the Pacific, into rivers, over the Andes, or simply into unmarked mass graves in the Desert of Atacama. According to the report, the state failed in its "moral responsibility" to return those who were disappeared, executed, or tortured to death, to their loved ones. But for Zurita, such a "moral responsibility" extends beyond the scope of a civil society. The return of Hektor's body in the *Iliad* reflects "an ancestral and archaic gesture anchored in what is profoundly human." That is, to be human is to properly mourn our deceased beloved, and this simply requires that they be in close proximity so that we might look upon them. But what do language and poetic form have to do with such things? How might syllables, vowels, letters, rhythm, syntax, or grammar take on the matter of lost bodies? And, furthermore, how would such an undertaking recuperate some sense of what it means to be human? These questions motivate Zurita's life work, and I believe that he addresses them by developing poetry as a form of beholding, or facing, history's fallen. Such beholding, as in the case of Priam, involves loving despair, the need for physical closeness, and a longing for unity as constitutive of humanity itself. Here I consider these grounding elements of Zurita's poetry from the 1970s to the present as well as how they have guided the selection and translation found in *Sky Below*.

Purgatorio (*Purgatory*; 1979), Zurita's first volume of poems, represents the cultural, physical, and emotional wreckage from which he draws to search for new combinations of language and forms that might speak to the Chilean coup's ferocity. In this inaugural work of a trilogy that includes *Anteparaíso* (*Anteparadise*, 1984) and *La vida nueva* (*New Life*, 1994), the poet gathers an archive of distinct representational fields such as a government issued photo ID, an encephalogram, a psychiatric report, mathematics and geometry, the Christian Bible, Buddhism, and Dante Alighieri's *Divine Comedy*. Indeed, Dante's masterpiece is as structurally foundational to Zurita's oeuvre as it is to his sense of language, kin, and love. Josefina Pessolo, or "Veli," Zurita's Italian grandmother, recited the poem to him as a child, and its themes of redemption, spiritual passage, and human suffering vis-à-vis the divine course through his life's work. At *Purgatory's* center, the poetic voice traverses Chile's Desert of Atacama, the most arid region on earth, through a shifting, converging, and expanding first person singular that is at once mad and lucid, whore and saint, broken and enlightened. In "The Desert of Atacama VII," the reader is invoked to participate in this plural voice and witness the disaster of "our loneliness" in the desert:

     i. Let's look then at the Desert of Atacama

     ii. Let's look at our loneliness in the desert

So that desolate before these forms the landscape becomes
a cross extended over Chile and the loneliness of my form
then sees the redemption of the other forms: my own
Redemption in the Desert

     iii. Then who would speak of the redemption of my form

     iv. Who would tell of the desert's loneliness

So that my form begins to touch your form and your form
that other form like that until all of Chile is nothing but
one form with open arms: a long form crowned with thorns

     v. Then the Cross will be nothing but the opening arms
       of my form

vi. We will then be the Crown of Thorns in the Desert

vii. Then   nailed form to form   like a Cross
     extended over Chile we will have seen forever
     the Final Solitary Breath of the Desert of Atacama

On this broad cross, crowned with thorns, Zurita frees Christ from his own narrative, that is, the political and religious sacrifice his father demanded of him. "So that my form begins to touch your form and your form that other form" imagines a shared recognition of individual as well as collective suffering. Convergence yields redemption as opposed to individual sacrifice, which yields an unbearable loneliness. Here Zurita also begins to unbind the Christ figure from the religious language and imagery of Christianity in which he, we, and the Spanish language is embedded. The void left by such a release is replaced by the image of human forms that touch one another interminably.

As I noted in the 2009 translation of *Purgatory*, "form" in the poem above represents the Chilean Spanish word *facha*, which has a range of interpretive possibilities. *Facha* first refers to an individual's "aspect," "aura," "image," or "look." I avoided these last words because in English they strongly recall the fashion industry and marketing. *Facha* also can refer to arrogance or haughtiness, inciting a Chilean to critically state, "¡Pero qué facha!" In English, phrases such as "What poor form!" or "How dare he?" demonstrate comparable sentiments. I chose "form," from the Latin *forma* or "to mold," to index as much the physical aspects or aura of an individual's body as the piecing together of registers, texts, objects, and representational fields found throughout *Purgatory*. Furthermore, through assonance, "form" manages an analogical purpose as it pulls together "[c]rown," "[t]horn," "[c]ross," "arms," and "forever." Nonetheless, "form" does not directly reflect *facha's* important etymological implications. *Facha* comes from the Italian *faccia* and the Latin *facia*, which in Spanish gave way to *faz* and, in English, *face*. Thus, on the one hand, the word's origins reflect Zurita's emphasis upon his own face throughout his oeuvre, beginning with *Purgatory* itself, whose frontispiece shows his cheek scarred by a self-inflicted wound. On the other hand, in Chilean Spanish *facha* extends the properties of the face to include the particular gestures and attributes of an individual's entire body. Zurita prompts us to come face to face as well as body to body with his and one another's wounds. We converge with the author *as the text* as well as one another to become a "cross extended over Chile."

But at the poem's center, what makes this intersection of *fachas*, faces, bodies, and forms possible, is proximity and *tocar* (touch). Susan Stewart has suggested that poetry itself is a "[f]ace-to-face" form that "bring[s] forward a desire to touch, a compulsion to be in proximity to the material of the work of art even as [it] require[s] the receiver to orbit between absorption and withdrawal."[4] Similarly, Francine Masiello notes that "the poem . . . offers a tactile and concrete space. From the poem's surface — its placement on the blank page, the construction of stanzas, the disorder of a strange sound that appeals to the ear and to touch simultaneously — we sustain tactility of the poem; its material is offered to us."[5] Stewart and Masiello help us think about poetry as a genre that incites touch as much through its form on the page as through language techniques that, in appealing to the ear, appeal to the entire body.

In like manner, Emmanuel Levinas extends the qualities of the human face to the body along with speech, discourse, and the work of art in his attempt to understand how the face might foreclose the possibility of violence. He begins by identifying the face's particular irreducibility, explaining that "completely naked . . . [the face] signifies itself."[6] The unique contours, gestures, and lines of each face willingly and unwillingly express the multiplicity of its presence.[7] This presence is as contemporary as it is infinite in that it figures the extraordinary complexity, emotions, desires, fears, and contradictions of its own body as well as all the genetic and experiential material of the bodies that have preceded it. Thus, in Zurita's poem, the cross of *fachas* yokes the particular and present with the communal, multiple and infinite.

Precisely because a face "signifies itself," Levinas believed it defies its own destruction. Violence toward another person involves as much brute force as an imposed deferral of signification. If I say to you, "your importance lies elsewhere, in your value as human capital," for example, I deny that your meaning lies simply in your presence. In the Chilean context, the reduction to capital of what is human is represented by the aggressive imposition of unprecedented free-market strategies upon the Chilean people.[8] Levinas then broadens the face's irreducibility and implicit subversive potential to include the work of art: "Can things take on a face?," he asks; "Is not art an activity that lends faces to things?"

Similarly, Zurita believes in the unity of life and art. In the late 1970s, he founded the Colectivo de Acciones de Arte (CADA) along with the writer Diamela Eltit, the sociologist Fernando Barcells, and the visual artists Lotty Rosenfeld and Juan Castillo. CADA performed a series of art actions and protests in public spaces—including the sky—that incited individuals to fuse art with political activism.[9] What Zurita began working toward is the idea that an individual's life is itself a work of art, and the work of art is the human face and body in form, the *facha*. Thus, Zurita would suggest that the coming together of these multifarious *fachas*, as faces and bodies, as poetry and art, has the capacity to defy the full range of a state's military and economic ferocity. Such a political and ethical possibility is ultimately grounded in an aesthetic appeal to touch. Touch is the beginning and end of closeness; of poetry; speech, as Levinas suggests; and art itself. In sum, touch is the beginning of what is human, and to deny such a thing at life's end is the ultimate atrocity. For Priam to "behold" his dead son, in Richard Lattimore's beautiful translation, is to "thoroughly touch" him, because this is what the word *bihaldan*, from the Old English, means.

I would like to further underscore this point regarding formal and human unity through touch by returning for a moment to our reading of the *Iliad*. How are we to understand Apollo's divine intervention within the context of the cadaver's return? Here the god suppresses the catastrophes of history; he erases marks that speak the victim's body, that is, the physical signs of the state's abuse. However, as Apollo makes the son's figure bearable to Priam and the conquered people's gaze, he recovers what is sacred for the desecrated and reveals human form among ruins. Zurita's language is grounded precisely in what Apollo rubs out: the physical and emotional lacerations of history's vanquished. But he simultaneously opens a space for the body's wholeness and even its resurrection. For example, in poem "X" of *Anteparadise*, Zurita writes, "Because even though all scars can't be rubbed out / and you can still see / the arms burned / The burns the scars they also / lift themselves as one alone from the bodies and sing." On the one hand, this language speaks from breaking skin and wreckage; there are no totalizing gestures, and chronological time bottoms out. On the other, Zurita challenges these postmodern symptoms by establishing a stable definition of humanity found in the persistent attempt to speak the body's experience through poetic form despite its destruction. Therein lies Zurita's complex sense of human agency and subjectivity: the scars, the burns themselves get up as "one alone" to sing. And just as poetic form sings the body's experience that is the person's life, that life constitutes a work of art, a unity in and of itself.

By the time *Purgatory* was published in 1979, Ignacio Valente, an influential critic, had identified Zurita as an important writer among Enrique Lihn, Armando Uribe, and Jorge Teiller, Chile's well-established literary elite.[10] Although the young Zurita received official, public recognition, his economic situation, like that of most Chileans, remained extremely precarious. With the assistance of Editores Asociados, the publishers of *Anteparadise*, in 1984 Zurita cobbled together funds to write a poem in the sky over Queens, New York. This monumental performance, the first of its kind, was dedicated to Latino populations in the United States. Images of the blue event are found throughout the book, and we have included a selection in this volume. Written with five planes, the poem, "Mi Dios es" ("My God Is"), figures a dominant word ("GOD") that is then displaced:

MY GOD IS HUNGER   MY GOD IS CHICANO

MY GOD IS SNOW   MY GOD IS CANCER

MY GOD IS NO   MY GOD IS EMPTINESS

MY GOD IS REGRET   MY GOD IS WOUND . . .

Here meaning falls away with the repetition of language sounds: MY GOD IS MY GOD IS MY GODISMYGODISMYGODISMYGODIS. This dissolution of "MY GOD IS" into sound results in the foregrounding of the diversifying series of nouns—"HUNGER," "CHICANO," "SNOW," and so on. Thus, what the poem ultimately expresses is humanity in its divergent multiplicity: "MY GOD IS ALL OF YOU." For Zurita, the representation of what is human necessarily involves the removal of the idea of God or any fixed ideology as an axis of knowledge, meaning, and power. Read from the earth, "My God Is" functions as an inverse prayer whose purpose is to figure the human face. That is, instead of the conferral of human characteristics through prosopopoeia onto a faceless entity, which in this case is God, here skywriting defines humanity in its range of common emotional, physical and political tribulations.

Across his extraordinary oeuvre, Zurita continues to rework the representational axes along which we understand language, power, religion, history, and love. *Canto a su amor desaparecido (Song for His Disappeared*

Love, 1985) delineates the geography of the Americas as niches containing the conquest, the massacre of indigenous populations, the slave trade, and thwarted political movements. The poem begins in the present of "concrete warehouses," where thousands of prisoners were held and tortured during the Chilean and many other twentieth-century Latin American dictatorships. The dead speak as they break apart, as they recall their torturers, as they face history and the nations born through their slaughter, as they still, nonetheless, seek love and the simplicity of touch. Pablo Neruda had already rewritten the history of the Americas from the perspective of the oppressed in his masterpiece *Canto general* (1950). However, while Neruda maintained the ability to sing for the fallen, Zurita's poetic voice disintegrates among those fallen. The breakdown of the first-person singular becomes a piercing love howl as the foundation of song and history at the poem's end.

Published after the fall of the Pinochet regime and redemocratization, the third book of the *Purgatory* trilogy, *New Life* (1994), begins in 1983 with the dreams and testimonies of peasants occupying immense parcels of land. Recalling an effort begun by the Chilean government several years before the coup to establish subsistence farming in massive, unused private territories, these testimonies are remnants of a crushed social, spiritual, emotional and economic dream. In *New Life* Zurita persists in writing the history of the Americas as he more ardently personifies the landscape—the oceans, the Andes, rivers, pastures, cliffs—building upon Gabriela Mistral's anguished poetic landscapes. The more than 300-page volume ends with "ni pena ni miedo" ("no pain no fear"), a poem Zurita inscribed with bulldozers into the rough sands of the Desert of Atacama in 1993. The two-mile geoglyph, which we have included at the end of *Sky Below*, converges language, landscape, and again, the figuration of the human face through the act of reading. Zurita projects the closeness that writing and reading demand through mouth, eyes, and ears, onto the landscape so that it become the page upon which we might imagine the intimate marks of our common existence.

While *Poemas militantes* (*Militant Poems*, 2000) represents Zurita's renewed hope in the possibility of a democratic government to reinvigorate the political efforts of the pre-Pinochet era, *INRI* (2003) speaks to the utter loss of that hope. In 2002, President Ricardo Lagos announced what the landscapes of Chile and military collaborators already knew: that the bodies of the disappeared were irrecuperable. *INRI* is Zurita's response to that disclosure. This epitaph, which stands for *Iesus Nazarenus Rex Iudaeorum* ("Jesus of Nazareth, King of the Jews"), recalls Nicanor Parra's antipoetry in its unrelenting sarcasm, its brutal sense of humor that is the irony of a military state. While previous texts maintain the momentum of narrative force, *INRI* represents the reified stillness of its title. Here Zurita memorializes the details of an individual's last moments as he is overcome by blows, as she is pushed down by the weight of dirt, or stones and others, as both descend into landscapes becoming those landscapes. At the center of what is perhaps Zurita's most devastating volume is "The Descent," a poem that begins with the words, "Te palpo, te toco." Here Zurita makes use of the indirect object (*te*), as opposed to the first person singular (*yo*), to converge "you" and "I" with the verbs "feel" (*palpo*) and "touch" (*toco*), despite the body's disintegration and descent. That is, even though history points to the destruction and disintegration of human bodies, our continual longing for one another constitutes a stable point of reference, a unity in the face of disintegration. Indeed, *INRI* speaks not only to the final moments of a person's crushed life; the book establishes history as the conditions of those last moments.

In *Zurita* (2011), a tour de force running more than 700 pages, the poet is most explicit in his merging of life and art. The book speaks in its sheer size to the inexhaustible act of mourning through language, but also to the inexhaustible nature of love. Here the poetic voice traverses time in three sections—"Your Broken Afternoon," "Your Broken Night," and "Your Broken Dawn"—that intersect "you," the reader, with the breadth of world history, a list of Chilean detention centers, testimonies, dreams, Native American indigenous languages and cosmogonies, Akira Kurosawa, Shakespeare, Pink Floyd, and the cliffs that look to the Pacific. Extending through *Zurita's* massive volume like a spinal column is a series of thirty-two poems, each called "Cielo abajo," or "Sky Below." This volume of selected works takes its name from these poems. Zurita has explained that "cielo abajo" is "something where the sky comes together with the earth, at the horizon . . . it's viewing a panorama that's far off, but precisely because of this, because viewed from the distance, the image is wider; it has greater breadth."[11] *Sky Below* culminates in images of a project that Zurita has envisioned but has yet to realize: the inscription of a poem called "Verás" ("You Will See") into the cliffs that overlook the Pacific. While poems such as "My God Doesn't Look   My God Doesn't Hear   My God Is Not" announce a faceless and thus inexistent God, "You Will See" calls us to be human. That is, the poem imagines a moment of paradise in the horizon, a moment in which we might behold, thoroughly touch and properly mourn what our world's silent landscapes have received on account of political, religious, military and economic ferocity: history's disappeared and beloved.

Anna Deeny Morales
Washington, D.C., 2016

Notes

EPIGRAPHS: Homer, *Iliad*, trans. Richard Lattimore, bk. 24, ll. 553–55; Raúl Zurita, "De la memoria y el sueño" ("From the Memory and Dream"), *Catálogo del Museo de la Memoria y los Derechos Humanos* (Santiago: Midia, 2011), 28.

1. See Peter Kornbluh, *The Pinochet File: A Declassified Dossier on Atrocity and Accountability* (New York and London: The New Press, 2003).

2. See the *Report of the Chilean National Commission for Truth and Reconciliation* (Rettig Report, 1991), available at http://www.usip.org; and the *Report of the Chilean National Commission on Political Imprisonment and Torture* (Valech Report, 2005), available at http://www.archivochile.com/Derechos_humanos/com_valech/Informe_complementario.pdf, and http://www.usip.org/publications/commission-of-inquiry-chile-03.

3. The Rettig Report was published under the government of President Patricio Aylwin. It states: "The decree defines those 'most serious violations' to be situations of those persons who disappeared after arrest, who were executed, or who were tortured to death, in which the moral responsibility of the state is compromised by acts of its agents or persons in their service, as well as kidnappings and attempts on the life of persons committed by individuals for political reasons" (42).

4. Susan Stewart. "Facing, Touch, and Vertigo," in her *Poetry and the Fate of the Senses.* (Chicago: University of Chicago Press, 2002), 161. Here Stewart draws from Harry Berger's idea of the "shuttle of perception" developed in "The System of Early Modern Painting," *Representations* 62 (spring 1998): 43.

5. Francine Masiello. "Poesía, sensación y ritmo," in her *El cuerpo de la voz (poesía, ética y cultura).* (Buenos Aires: Beatriz Verbo Editora, 2013): "[E]l poema . . . ofrece un espacio táctil y concreto. De la superficie del poema—su disposición sobre la página en blanco, la construcción de las estrofas, el desajuste de un sonido extraño que apela al oído y al tacto

simultáneamente—sostenemos la tactilidad del poema; su material se nos ofrece" (55). (My translation.)

6. Emmanuel Levinas, "Is Ontology Fundamental?" (1951), in Levinas, *Basic Philosophical Writings*, ed. Adriaan T. Peperzak, Simon Critchley, and Robert Bernasconi (Bloomington: Indiana University Press, 1996), 10.

7. Ibid.

8. In an article that cost him his life, Orlando Letelier was one of the first to point out that in the United States, the Chilean military regime was largely represented and perceived as the hapless, as opposed to necessary, collateral damage of the opening up of Chile's primary resources to neo-liberalism and a global market. The blueprint for a "free market" in Chile mapped out by Milton Freidman and other economists associated with the University of Chicago (known as the "Chicago Boys") was the mask of an unprecedented experiment in unrestrained capitalism. See "The Chicago Boys in Chile: Economic Freedom's Economic Toll," *The Nation*, Aug. 28, 1976.

9. For images of CADA's work, see http://www.memoriachilena.cl/602/ w3-article-98248.html, and http://hemisphericinstitute.org/hemi/en/ modules/itemlist/category/100-cada. See also Robert Neustadt, *Cada día: la creación de un arte social* (Santiago: Editorial Cuarto Propio, 2001).

10. See Ignacio Valente, "El poeta Zurita" (1975), and "Zurita entre los grandes" (1977), in his *Veinticinco años de crítica* (Santiago: Zig-Zag, 1992).

11. Raúl Zurita, e-mail to Anna Deeny Morales, September 3, 2015. "Cielo abajo es para mí como algo que se sitúa donde el cielo se junta con la tierra, en el horizonte, es algo que está al final de lo que vemos, es como ver un panorama que está lejos, al final, pero que por eso mismo, por ser visto desde la distancia, es la visión más amplia, más ancha."

SKY

BELOW

DE *PURGATORIO*

FROM *PURGATORY*

mis amigos creen que
estoy muy mala
porque quemé mi mejilla

my   friends   think
I'm   a   sick   woman
because I burned my cheek

EN EL MEDIO DEL CAMINO

IN THE MIDDLE OF THE ROAD

EGO SUM

Me llamo Raquel
estoy en el oficio
desde hace varios
años. Me encuentro
en la mitad de
mi vida. Perdí
el camino.—

QUI SUM

My name is Rachel
I've been in the same
business for many
years. I'm in the
middle of my life.
I lost my way. —

XXII

Destrocé mi cara tremenda
frente al espejo

te amo—me dije—te amo
Te amo a más que nada en el mundo

XXII

I smashed my sickening face
in the mirror

I love you—I said—I love you
I love you more than anything in the world

LXIII

Hoy soñé que era Rey
me ponían una piel a manchas blancas y negras
Hoy mujo con mi cabeza a punto de caer
mientras las campanadas fúnebres de la iglesia
dicen que va a la venta la leche

LXIII

Today I dreamed that I was King
they were dressing me in black-and-white spotted pelts
Today I moo with my head about to fall
as the church bells' mournful clanging
says that milk goes to market

DESIERTOS

DESERTS

COMO UN SUEÑO

Claro: este es el Desierto
de Atacama   buena cosa   no
valía ni tres chauchas llegar
allí y no has visto el
Desierto de Atacama—oye:
lo viste allá cierto? bueno
si no lo has visto anda de
una vez y no me jodas

LAPSUS Y ENGAÑOS SE LLAMAN MI PROPIA MENTE EL
DESIERTO DE CHILE

LIKE A DREAM

Of course: this is the Desert
of Atacama   impressive   it
didn't cost a dime to get there
and you haven't seen the
Desert of Atacama—listen:
you saw it out there didn't
you? well if you haven't seen
it just go once and for all
and leave me the fuck alone

LAPSES AND DECEITS ARE CALLED MY OWN MIND THE
DESERT OF CHILE

QUIEN PODRÍA LA ENORME DIGNIDAD DEL
DESIERTO DE ATACAMA COMO UN PÁJARO
SE ELEVA SOBRE LOS CIELOS APENAS
EMPUJADO POR EL VIENTO

WHO COULD THE ENORMOUS DIGNITY OF
THE DESERT OF ATACAMA LIKE A BIRD
IT ELEVATES ITSELF OVER THE SKIES BARELY
PRESSED BY THE WIND

I

A LAS INMACULADAS LLANURAS

  i. Dejemos pasar el infinito del Desierto de Atacama

  ii. Dejemos pasar la esterilidad de estos desiertos

Para que desde las piernas abiertas de mi madre se
levante una Plegaria que se cruce con el infinito del
Desierto de Atacama y mi madre no sea entonces sino
un punto de encuentro en el camino

  iii. Yo mismo seré entonces una Plegaria encontrada
      en el camino

  iv. Yo mismo seré las piernas abiertas de mi madre

Para cuando vean alzarse ante sus ojos los desolados
paisajes del Desierto de Atacama mi madre se concentre
en gotas de agua y sea la primera lluvia en el desierto

  v. Entonces veremos aparecer el Infinito del Desierto

  vi. Dado vuelta desde sí mismo hasta dar con las piernas
      de mi madre

  vii. Entonces sobre el vacío del mundo se abrirá
      completamente el verdor infinito del Desierto de
      Atacama

I

TO THE IMMACULATE PLAINS

i. Let's let the infinity of the Desert of Atacama pass

ii. Let's let the sterility of these deserts pass

So that from the spread-open legs of my mother a Prayer
rises that intersects the infinity of the Desert of Atacama
and my mother is then nothing but a meeting point on
the road

iii. Then I myself will be a Prayer found on the road

iv. I myself will be the spread-open legs of my mother

So that when they see raised up before their eyes the
desolate landscapes of the Desert of Atacama my mother
will be concentrated in drops of water as the first rain of
the desert

v. Then we'll see the Infinity of the Desert appear

vi. Turned around itself until meeting my mother's
legs

vii. Then over the world's emptiness the infinite
green of the Desert of Atacama will open
completely

EL DESIERTO DE ATACAMA II

Helo allí   Helo allí
suspendido en el aire
El Desierto de Atacama

i. Suspendido   sobre el cielo de Chile   diluyéndose
entre auras

ii. Convirtiendo esta vida y la otra en el mismo
Desierto de Atacama   áurico   perdiéndose en el
aire

iii. Hasta que finalmente no haya cielo sino Desierto
de Atacama y todos veamos entonces nuestras
propias pampas fosforescentes carajas
encumbrándose en el horizonte

THE DESERT OF ATACAMA II

There   it   is   There
suspended   in   the   air
The   Desert   of   Atacama

   i. Suspended   over the sky of Chile   dissolving
     amid auras

 ii. Converting this life and the other into the same
     Desert of Atacama   luminous   losing itself in the
     air

iii. Until finally there's not sky but only Desert of
     Atacama and then all of us will see our own fucked
     phosphorescent pampas soaring in the horizon

EL DESIERTO DE ATACAMA III

i. Los desiertos de atacama son azules

ii. Los desiertos de atacama no son azules   ya ya dime
lo que quieras

iii. Los desiertos de atacama no son azules porque por
allá no voló el espíritu de J. Cristo que era un perdido

iv. Y si los desiertos de atacama fueran azules todavía
podrían ser el Oasis Chileno para que desde todos
los rincones de Chile contentos viesen flamear por
el aire   las azules pampas del Desierto de Atacama

THE DESERT OF ATACAMA III

    i. The deserts of atacama are blue

   ii. The deserts of atacama are not blue   go ahead say
       what you will

  iii. The deserts of atacama are not blue because
       out there J. Christ's spirit didn't fly he was a lost man

  iv. And if the deserts of atacama were blue still
       they could be the Chilean Oasis so that from every
       corner of Chile gladly you'd see flaming through
       the air   the blue pampas of the Desert of Atacama

VII

EL DESIERTO DE ATACAMA

i. Miremos entonces el Desierto de Atacama

ii. Miremos nuestra soledad en el desierto

Para que desolado frente a estas fachas el paisaje devenga
una cruz extendida sobre Chile y la soledad de mi facha
vea entonces el redimirse de las otras fachas: mi propia
Redención en el Desierto

iii. Quién diría entonces del redimirse de mi facha

iv. Quién hablaría de la soledad del desierto

Para que mi facha comience a tocar tu facha y tu facha
a esa otra facha y así hasta que todo Chile no sea sino
una sola facha con los brazos abiertos: una larga facha
coronada de espinas

v. Entonces la Cruz no será sino el abrirse de brazos
de mi facha

vi. Nosotros seremos entonces la Corona de Espinas
del Desierto

vii. Entonces   clavados facha con facha   como una Cruz
extendida sobre Chile habremos visto para siempre
el Solitario Expirar del Desierto de Atacama

VII

THE DESERT OF ATACAMA

    i. Let's look then at the Desert of Atacama

    ii. Let's look at our loneliness in the desert

So that desolate before these forms the landscape becomes
a cross extended over Chile and the loneliness of my form
then sees the redemption of the other forms: my own
Redemption in the Desert

    iii. Then who would speak of the redemption of my form

    iv. Who would tell of the desert's loneliness

So that my form begins to touch your form and your form
that other form like that until all of Chile is nothing but
one form with open arms: a long form crowned with thorns

    v. Then the Cross will be nothing but the opening arms
       of my form

    vi. We will then be the Crown of Thorns in the Desert

    vii. Then   nailed form to form   like a Cross
       extended over Chile we will have seen forever
       the Final Solitary Breath of the Desert of Atacama

ÁREAS VERDES

GREEN AREAS

Han visto extenderse estos pastos infinitos?

I. Han visto extenderse esos pastos infinitos
   donde las vacas huyendo desaparecen
   reunidas   ingrávidas   delante de ellos?

II. No hay domingos para la vaca:
    mugiendo despierta en un espacio vacío
    babeante   gorda   sobre esos pastos imaginarios

Have you seen these infinite pastures extend themselves?

I. Have you seen those infinite pastures extend themselves
   where the cows fleeing disappear
   reunited   weightless   before them?

II. There are no Sundays for the cow:
    lowing awake in a hollow space
    drooling   heavy   over those imaginary pastures

Comprended las fúnebres manchas de la vaca
los vaqueros
lloran frente a esos nichos

I. Esta vaca es una insoluble paradoja
   pernocta bajo las estrellas
   pero se alimenta de logos
   y sus manchas finitas son símbolos

II. Esa otra en cambio odia los colores:
    se fue a pastar a un tiempo
    donde el único color que existe es el negro

Ahora los vaqueros no saben qué hacer con
esa vaca pues sus manchas no son otra cosa
que la misma sombra de sus perseguidores

Comprehend the cow's woeful stains
the cowboys
weep before those recesses

I. This cow is an insoluble paradox
   she spends the night under the stars
   but nourishes herself of logos
   and her finite stains are symbols

II. That other one however hates colors:
    she went to graze one time
    where the only color that exists is black

Now the cowboys don't know what to do with
that cow because her stains are nothing
but the shadow itself of her persecutors

Quién daría por esas auras manchadas?

Quién daría algo por esas auras manchadas que las
vacas mugiendo dejan libres en los blancos espacios
no regidos de la muerte de sus perseguidores?

   I. La fuga de esas vacas es en la muerte no regida del
      vaquero   Por eso no mugen y son simbólicas

   II. Iluminadas   en la muerte de sus perseguidores
      Agrupando símbolos

   III. Retornando de esos blancos espacios no regidos
      a través de los blancos espacios de la muerte de Ud.
      que está loco   al revés   delante de ellas

Daría Ud. algo por esas azules auras que las vacas
mugiendo dejan libres   cerradas   y donde Ud. está
en su propio más allá muerto   imaginario   regresando
de esas persecuciones?

Who would give for those stained auras?

Who would give something for those stained auras
that the lowing cows leave free in the white spaces
not patrolled by the death of their persecutors?

   I. The fugue of those cows is in the death not
      patrolled by the cowboy   That's why they don't
      low and are symbolic

   II. Enlightened   in the death of their persecutors
      Grouping symbols

  III. Returning from those non-patrolled white spaces
      through those white spaces of the death of you
      who is mad   inside out   before them

Would you give something for those blue auras that
the cows lowing let free   enclosed   and where you're
in your own beyond   dead   imaginary   returning
from those persecutions?

MI AMOR DE DIOS

MY LOVE OF GOD

LOS CAMPOS DEL HAMBRE

Áreas N = El Hambre de Mi Corazón

Áreas N = Campos N El Hambre de

Áreas N =

y el Hambre Infinita de Mi Corazón

THE FIELDS OF HUNGER

Areas N = The Hunger of My Heart

Areas N = Fields N The Hunger of

Areas N =

and the Infinite Hunger of My Heart

LAS LLANURAS DEL DOLOR

eli

eli

y dolor

THE PLAINS OF PAIN

eli

eli

and pain

MI AMOR DE DIOS

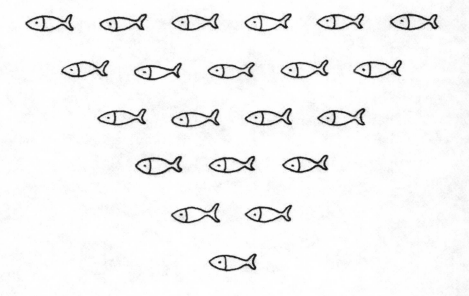

MY LOVE OF GOD

LA VIDA NUEVA

NEW LIFE

PARADISO

2640

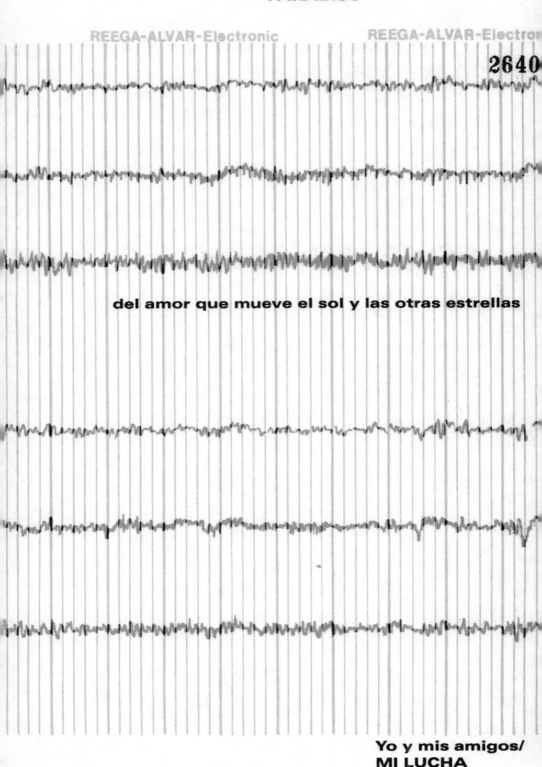

del amor que mueve el sol y las otras estrellas

Yo y mis amigos/
MI LUCHA

PARADISO

264080

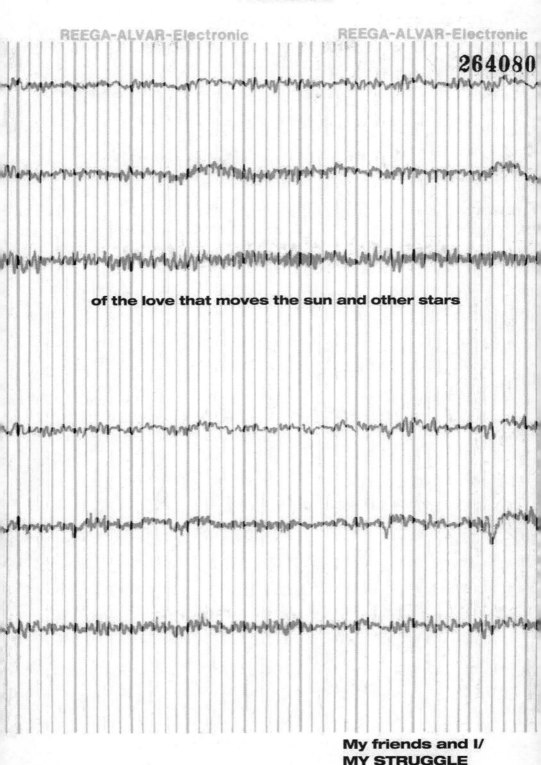

of the love that moves the sun and other stars

My friends and I/
MY STRUGGLE

DE *ANTEPARAÍSO*

FROM *ANTEPARADISE*

LA VIDA NUEVA

MI DIOS ES HAMBRE

MI DIOS ES NIEVE

MI DIOS ES NO

MI DIOS ES DESENGAÑO

MI DIOS ES CARROÑA

MI DIOS ES PARAÍSO

MI DIOS ES PAMPA

MI DIOS ES CHICANO

MI DIOS ES CÁNCER

MI DIOS ES VACÍO

MI DIOS ES HERIDA

MI DIOS ES GHETTO

MI DIOS ES DOLOR

MI DIOS ES

MI AMOR DE DIOS

—escrito en el cielo—
Nueva York—Junio 1982

NEW LIFE

MY GOD IS HUNGER

MY GOD IS SNOW

MY GOD IS NO

MY GOD IS REGRET

MY GOD IS CARION

MY GOD IS PARADISE

MY GOD IS PAMPA

MY GOD IS CHICANO

MY GOD IS CANCER

MY GOD IS EMPTINESS

MY GOD IS WOUND

MY GOD IS GHETTO

MY GOD IS PAIN

MY GOD IS

MY LOVE OF GOD

—written in the sky—
New York—June 1982

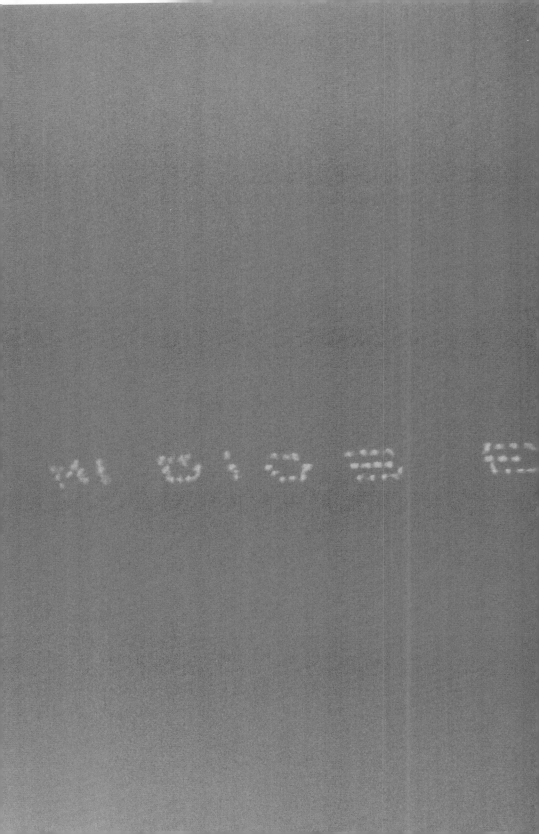

LAS UTOPÍAS

UTOPIAS

LAS PLAYAS DE CHILE I

No eran esos los chilenos destinos
que lloraron   alejándose toda la playa se
iba haciendo una pura llaga en sus ojos

No eran esas playas que encontraron sino más bien el carear
del cielo frente a sus ojos   albo   como si no fuera de ellos
en todo Chile espejeando las abiertas llagas que lavaban

    i. Empapado de lágrimas arrojó sus vestimentas al agua

   ii. Desnudo lo hubieran visto acurrucarse hecho un ovillo
      sobre sí   tembloroso   con las manos cubriéndose el
      pulular de sus heridas

  iii. Como un espíritu   lo hubieran ustedes visto cómo se
      abrazó a sí mismo   lívido   gimiente   mientras se le
      iba esfumando el color del cielo en sus ojos

Porque no eran esas playas que encontraron sino el volcarse
de todas las llagas sobre ellos   blancas   dolidas   sobre sí
cayéndoles como una bendición que les fijara en sus pupilas

  iv. Porque hasta lo que nunca fue renació alborando por
      esas playas

   v. Ese era el resplandor de sus propias llagas abiertas en
      la costa

  vi. Ese era el relumbrar de todas las playas que recién allí
      le saludaron la lavada visión de sus ojos

Porque no eran esas las costas que encontraron sino sus propias
llagas extendiéndose hasta ser la playa donde todo Chile comenzó
a arrojar sus vestimentas al agua   radiantes   esplendorosos
lavando frente a otros los bastardos destinos que lloraron

THE BEACHES OF CHILE I

Those were not the Chileans destinies
they wept   withdrawing itself the whole
beach became an utter sore in their eyes

Those were not the beaches they found but the sky face
to face with their eyes   white dawn   as if not theirs
in the whole of Chile reflecting the open sores they washed

    i. Soaked in tears he threw his vestments to the water

    ii. Naked you'd have seen him huddled coiled upon
       himself   shaking   with his hands covered over
       the swarm at his wounds

    iii. Like a spirit   you all would've seen how he held
       his arms around himself   livid   howling   as the
       sky's hue vanished from his eyes

Because those were not beaches they found but the over-
spill of all sores on them   colorless   in pain   upon itself
falling over them like a blessing that he'd set in their pupils

    iv. Because even what never was was reborn dawning
       through those beaches

    v. This was the resplendence of his own open sores on
       the shore

    vi. This was the dazzle of all the beaches that having just
       arrived there received the cleansed vision of his eyes

Because those were not the shores they came upon but their
own sores extending themselves until being the beach where
the whole of Chile began to throw its vestments to the water
radiant   splendorous   washing in front of others the bastard
destinies they wept

LAS PLAYAS DE CHILE VII

Muchos podrían haberlo llamado Utopía
porque sus habitantes viven solamente
de lo que comparten, de los trabajos
en las faenas de la pesca y del trueque.
Ellos habitan en cabañas de tablas a las
orillas del mar y más que con hombres
se relacionan con sus ánimas y santos
que guardan para calmar la furia de las
olas. Nadie habla, pero en esos días en
que la tormenta rompe, el silencio de sus
caras se hace más intenso que el ruido
del mar y no necesitan rezar en voz alta
porque es el universo entero su catedral

i. Solitarias   todas las playas de Chile se iban elevando como
una visión que les bañara las pupilas

ii. En que Chile fue el hijo lanzándonos un adiós desde esas
playas y nosotros el horizonte que lo despedía   eclipsado
clavándole los ojos

iii. Y en que lejanas ya no hubo playas sino la solitaria visión
donde los muertos lanzaron el adiós que nos clavaba en
sus miradas renacidos   vivísimos   como corderos bajo
el cielo emocionado en que la patria llorando volvió a
besar a sus hijos

THE BEACHES OF CHILE VII

Many could have called it Utopia
because the people only live on what
they share, on the work of fisherfolk
and barter. They lodge in wood cabins
at the edge of the sea and more than
with men they commune with saints and
souls they keep to still the fury of waves.
No one speaks, but those days the storm
breaks, the silence of their faces becomes
more intense than the sea's rumble and
they don't have to pray out loud because
the entire universe is their cathedral

i. Alone   all of Chile's beaches went on rising like a
   vision that would bathe their pupils

ii. In which Chile was the son calling out to us goodbye
    from those beaches and we were the horizon that
    saw him off   eclipsed   nailing his eyes

iii. And in that they were far there weren't beaches anymore
     but the solitary vision where the dead called out the
     goodbye that nailed us to their gazes reborn   so alive
     like lambs below the sky moved because the fatherland
     weeping kissed his children again

LAS PLAYAS DE CHILE X

Yo lo vi soltando los remos acurrucarse
contra el fondo del bote   La playa aún
se espejeaba en la opaca luz de sus ojos

La playa aún se espejeaba en sus ojos pero apenas como un territorio
irreal opacándole la mirada   alargado   evanescente   en un nuevo
Chile mojándoles las costas que creyeron

    i. Hecho un ánima sintió como se le iban soltando los remos
       de las manos

    ii. Empapado   toda la vida se le fue desprendiendo como si
       ella misma fuera los remos que se le iban yendo de entre
       los dedos

    iii. Incluso su propio aliento le sonó ajeno mientras se dejaba
       caer de lado   suavemente   como un copo de nieve
       contra las frágiles tablas que hasta allí lo llevaron

En que la playa nunca volvería a espejearse en sus ojos sino acaso
el relumbrar de un nuevo mundo que les fuera adhiriendo otra luz
en sus pupilas   empañadas   erráticas   alzándoles de frente el
horizonte que les arrasó de lágrimas la cara

    iv. Porque sólo allí la playa espejeó en sus ojos

    v. Recién entonces pudo sentir sobre sus mejillas el aire
       silbante de estas costas

    vi. Únicamente allí pudo llorar sin contenerse por esa playa
       que volvía a humedecerle la mirada

Porque la playa nunca se espejearía en sus ojos sino mejor en el
derramarse de todas las utopías como un llanto incontenible que se le
fuera desprendiendo del pecho   hirviente   desgarrado   despejando la
costa que Chile entero le vio adorarse en la iluminada de estos sueños

THE BEACHES OF CHILE X

I saw him let the oars go and huddle against
the bottom of the boat   The beach still
reflected itself in the clouded light of his eyes

The beach still reflected itself in his eyes but barely like an unreal
territory clouding his gaze   elongated   evanescent   in a new
Chile wetting the shores they believed

    i. A soul now he felt the oars as they slipped from his
       hands

    ii. Soaked   all life left rending as if she herself were
       the oars that slipped through his fingers

    iii. Even his own breath sounded unknown as he let him-
       self fall sideways   softly   like a snowflake   against
       the fragile boards that took him there

In that the beach would never return to reflect itself in his eyes until
perhaps the dazzle of a new world that would cling another light to
their pupils   drenched   erratic   in front of them lifting the horizon
that razed their faces with tears

    iv. Because only there the beach reflected in his eyes

    v. Just then could he feel on his cheeks the whistling air
       of those shores

    vi. It was there that he could weep without holding himself
       back through that beach that dampened his gaze again

Because the beach would never reflect itself in his eyes but
instead in the shedding of all utopias like an uncontainable
grieve rent from his chest   boiling   torn   clearing the shore
that all of Chile saw adore itself in the illuminance of those dreams

CORDILLERAS

CORDILLERAS

/CI/

Se hacía tarde ya cuando tomándome un hombro
me ordenó:
"Anda y mátame a tu hijo"
Vamos—le repuse sonriendo—¿me estás tomando
el pelo acaso?
"Bueno, si no quieres hacerlo es asunto tuyo,
pero recuerda quién soy, así que después no
te quejes"
Conforme—me escuché contestarle—¿y dónde
quieres que cometa ese asesinato?
Entonces, como si fuera el aullido del viento
quien hablase, El dijo:
"Lejos, en esas perdidas cordilleras de Chile"

/CI/

It was already getting late when he took
hold of my shoulder and ordered:
"Go and kill me your son"
Come on—I grinned—you're kidding,
right?
"Well, if you don't want to that's your
choice, but remember who I am, and then
don't you complain"
Willing—I heard myself answer him—and
where do you want this killing done?
Then, as if it were the wind howl that spoke,
He said:
"Far off, in those lost cordilleras of Chile"

Con la cara ensangrentada llamé a su puerta:
Podría ayudarme—le dije—tengo unos amigos
afuera
"Márchate de aquí—me contestó—antes de que
te eche a patadas"
Vamos—le observé—usted sabe que también
rechazaron a Jesús.
"Tú no eres El—me respondió—ándate o te
rompo la crisma. Yo no soy tu padre"
Por favor—le insistí—los tipos que están
afuera son hijos suyos . . .
"De acuerdo—contestó suavizándose—llévalos
a la tierra prometida"
Bien ¿pero dónde queda ese sitio?—pregunté—
Entonces, como si fuera una estrella la que
lo dijese, me respondió:
"Lejos, en esas perdidas cordilleras de Chile"

With my face blood-soaked I called at his door:
Could you help me—I said—I've got some
friends out here
"Go away—he replied—before I kick the
shit out of you"
Come on—I reminded him—sir you know they
also turned Jesus back.
"You're not Jesus—he answered—get or I'll
break your face. I'm not your father"
Please—I insisted—they're your sons . . .
"Fine—he said calming down—take them to
the promised land"
Okay, but where is that place?—I asked—
Then, as if it were a star that spoke, he
answered:
"Far off, in those lost cordilleras of Chile"

Despertado de pronto en sueños lo oí tras la
noche
"Oye Zurita—me dijo—toma a tu mujer y a tu
hijo y te largas de inmediato"
No macanees—le repuse—déjame dormir en
paz, soñaba con unas montañas que marcha . . .
"Olvida esas estupideces y apúrate—me urgió—
no vas a creer que tienes todo el tiempo del
mundo. El Duce se está acercando"
Escúchame—contesté—recuerda que hace
mucho ya que me tienes a la sombra, no
intentarás repetirme el cuento. Yo no soy José.
"Sigue la carretera y no discutas. Muy pronto
sabrás la verdad"
Está bien—le repliqué casi llorando—¿y dónde
podrá ella alumbrar tranquila?
Entonces, como si fuera la misma Cruz la que se
iluminase, El contestó:
"Lejos, en esas perdidas cordilleras de Chile"

Awoken suddenly from dreams I heard him
in the night
"Listen Zurita—he said—get your wife and
your son and leave now"
Don't screw with me—I said—let me sleep in
peace, I was dreaming about these mountains
that went . . .
"Forget that shit and get out of here"—he was
adamant—don't think you have so much time.
The Duce is closing in"
Listen—I said—remember that for a while
now you've kept me in the dark, don't try to
do it again. I'm not Joseph.
"Stay on this road and don't argue. Soon
you'll know the truth"
Fine—I said back almost weeping—and
where could she calmly have the child?
Then, as if the Cross itself illumined, He
responded:
"Far off, in those lost cordilleras of Chile"

PASTORAL

PASTORAL

PASTORAL

Chile entero es un desierto
sus llanuras se han mudado y sus ríos
están más secos que las piedras
No hay un alma que camine por sus calles
y sólo los malos
parecieran estar en todas partes

¡Ah si tan sólo tú me tendieras tus brazos
las rocas se derretirían al verte!

PASTORAL

Chile is all desert
her plains are gone and her rivers
more parched than stones
Not one soul walks through her streets
and only the evil
seem to be everywhere

Ah if you would just hold your arms out to me
were they to see you the rocks would thaw!

EL GRITO DE MARÍA

Quemados los praderíos crepitaron ardientes hasta volarse
en el grito de María   sobre el valle   llorándose el luto
como manchones de tizne que el mismo cielo ensombrecieron

    i. Ensombrecidos   un grito escucharon los valles que
       se quemaban

    ii. Sólo un grito fue el crepitar de aquellos pastos

    iii. Nada más que María fue el grito que Chile escuchó
       desflorándose sobre el campo

Porque todo Chile crepitó estremeciéndose para ya no ser
más que los pastos del grito de María   arrasados bajo el
cielo   desflorados   como tiña que hasta el aire evitara

    iv. Porque sólo pena salió del valle desflorado de
       María

    v. Así el grito fue la pascua ardida de Chile

    vi. Todo Chile gritó entonces desflorándose en las
       quemadas pascuas de sus valles

Desde donde los mismos cielos crepitaron hasta remachar
con un grito la desflorada pascua de María   ardida   de tiña
por los milenios llorando los quemados pastos de este luto

MARIA'S SCREAM

Burned the meadowlands crackled in flames until soaring
in Maria's scream   over the valley   weeping her own
grieve like huge soot stains that overshadowed the sky itself

   i. Overshadowed   a scream is what the burning
     valleys heard

   ii. One scream was the crackling of those valleys

   iii. No more than Maria was the scream that Chile heard
      deflowering its own self over the countryside

Because the whole of Chile crackled shuddering to no longer
be more than the pastures of Maria's scream   razed below
the sky   deflowered   like ringworm that even the air shuns

   iv. Because only sorrow came from Maria's deflowered
      valley

   v. Like that the scream was Chile's Christmas in flames

   vi. Then the whole of Chile screamed deflowering itself
      in the burned Christmas of its valleys

From where the same skies crackled until clinching with a scream
Maria's deflowered Christmas   in flames   of ringworm
through the millennia weeping the burned pastures of this grieve

TODO HA SIDO CONSUMADO

   i. Por última vez oigan entonces las llanuras

   ii. Miren por última vez los pastos que quedan

Porque quemados todos fueron el último grito que esos
valles repitieron   ardidos   de muerte   por los aires
llorándose hechos cenizas que se volaban

   iii. Porque nada volvió a florecer en los pastos
      consumados

   iv. Por eso hasta las cenizas se volaron con las
      arrasadas de estos pastos

Por donde Chile crepitó de muerte sobre sus valles y los
valles fueron allí el "consumado todo está" que gritaron
llorando a las alturas   abandonados   como una maldición
que les consumiera entera la vida en esos pastos

   v. Porque allí se vio ascender ardidos los valles sobre
     Chile

   vi. Por eso hasta las cenizas gritaban llorando "todo
     ha sido consumado"

   vii. Entonces   por última vez   como elevándose desde
      sus cenizas   sobre los cielos vieron arder los
      moribundos valles que todo Chile les lloraban

ALL HAS BEEN CONSUMED

   i. For the last time then hear the plains

   ii. Look one last time at what's left of the pastures

Because burned they were all the last scream that those
valleys repeated   in flames   of death   through the airs
weeping themselves made ashes that would blow away

   iii. Because nothing flowered again in the consumed
        pastures

   iv. That's why even the ashes blew away with the
        razings of these pastures

Through which Chile crackled of death over her valleys and
the valleys over there were "consumed it is all done" that
they screamed weeping to the heights   abandoned   like a
curse that would consume their whole life in those pastures

   v. Because out there the valleys in flames ascending
        were seen over Chile

   vi. That's why even the ashes screamed weeping "all
        has been consumed"

   vii. Then   for one last time   as if lifting itself up
        from its ashes   above the skies they saw on fire
        the dying valleys for which all Chile wept

II

Los pastos crecían cuando te encontré acurrucada
tiritando de frío entre los muros
Entonces te tomé
con mis manos lavé tu cara
y ambos temblamos de alegría cuando te pedí
que te vinieses conmigo
Porque ya la soledad no era
yo te vi llorar alzando hasta mí tus párpados quemados
Así vimos florecer el desierto
así escuchamos los pájaros de nuevo cantar
sobre las rocas de los páramos que quisimos
Así estuvimos entre los pastos crecidos
y nos hicimos uno y nos prometimos para siempre
Pero tú no cumpliste, tú te olvidaste
de cuando te encontré y no eras más que una esquirla
en el camino. Te olvidaste
y tus párpados y tus piernas se abrieron para otros
Por otros quemaste tus ojos
Se secaron los pastos y el desierto me fue el alma
como hierro al rojo sentí las pupilas
al mirarte manoseada por tus nuevos amigos
nada más que para enfurecerme
Pero yo te seguí queriendo
no me olvidé de ti y por todas parte pregunté
si te habían visto y te encontré de nuevo
para que de nuevo me dejaras
Todo Chile se volvió sangre al ver tus fornicaciones
Pero yo te seguí queriendo y volveré a buscarte
y nuevamente te abrazaré sobre la tierra reseca
para pedirte otra vez que seas mi mujer
Los pastos de Chile volverán a revivir
El desierto de Atacama florecerá de alegría
las playas cantarán y bailarán para cuando avergonzada
vuelvas conmigo para siempre
y yo te haya perdonado todo lo que me has hecho
¡hija de mi patria!

II

The pastures grew when I found you huddled
writhing from the cold between the walls
Then I took you in
with my hands I cleaned your face
and both we trembled of joy when
I asked you to come with me
Because there was no more loneliness
I saw you weep lifting your burned eyelids to me
That's how we saw the desert flower
that's how we listened again to the birds sing
above the rocks of those moors we loved
That's how we were among the overgrown pastures
and we became one and promised ourselves forever
But you broke your promise, you forgot
about when I found you and you were just a splinter
in the road. You forgot
and your eyes and legs they opened for others
You burned your eyes for others
The pastures dried up and the desert was my soul
my pupils red-hot irons
as I watched you felt up by your new friends
just to enrage me
But I still loved you
I didn't forget you and I asked all over the place
if they'd seen you and I found you again
just so you could leave me
All of Chile turned to blood seeing you sell yourself
But I still loved you and I will come back to look for you
and once again I'll hold you over the parched earth
and ask you to be my wife
The pastures of Chile will live once more
The desert of Atacama will flower with joy
and the beaches will sing and dance so that when ashamed
you return to me forever
and I will have forgiven all you've done to me
daughter of my country!

85

X

Yo sé que tú vives
yo sé ahora que tú vives y que tocada de luz
ya no entrará más en ti ni el asesino ni el tirano
ni volverán a quemarse los pastos sobre Chile
Abandonen entonces las cárceles
abandonen los manicomios y los cuarteles
que los gusanos abandonen la carroña
y los torturadores la mesa de los torturados
que abandone el sol los planetas que lo circundan
para que sólo de amor hable todo el universo
Que sólo de eso hablen los satélites y las radios
la noche y los eclipses
las barriadas y los campamentos
Que sólo de amor hablen hasta los orines y las heces
Porque está de novia la vista
y de casamentero el oído
porque volvieron a reverdecer los campos
y ella está ahora frente a mí
Griten entonces porque yo sé que tú vives
y por este Idilio se encuentran los perdidos
y los desollados vuelven a tener piel
Porque aunque no se borren todas las cicatrices
y todavía se distingan
las quemaduras en los brazos
También las quemaduras y las cicatrices
se levantan como una sola desde los cuerpos y cantan
Con cerros, cordilleras y valles
con dulces y mansos, muertos y vivos
cantando con todo cuanto vive esta prometida del amor
que puede florecer desiertos y glaciares

X

I know you live
I know now that you live and that touched by light
the assassin won't the tyrant won't ever get in you again
and the pastures over Chile won't burn again
So leave the prisons
leave insane asylums and encampments
let the worms leave the carrion
and the torturers the tables of the tortured
let the sun leave planets that surround it
so that the universe speak only of love
Let satellites and radios only speak to this
the night and eclipses
the ghettos and slums
even urine and feces only of love let them speak
Because our eyes are a bride
and our ears a matchmaker
because the fields became green again
and she's there in front of me
All of you cry out then because I know you live
and through this Idyll the lost are found
and the flayed have skin again
Because even though all scars can't be rubbed out
and you can still see
the arms burned
The burns the scars they also
lift themselves up as one alone from the bodies and sing
With hills, with cordilleras, with valleys
with the meek and mild, the living and the dead
singing with all as is alive this promised woman of love
that can bloom glaciers and deserts

IDILIO GENERAL

i. Abrácense entonces las llanuras de este vuelo

ii. Que cuanto vive se abrace inmaculado sobre estos
   pastos

Para que todo rubor Chile salga a mirarse por los valles
y cuanto vive vea entonces la paz que ellos se pidieron:
el verde inmaculado de estos pastos

iii. Porque volados lloraron de alegría sobre las
    llanuras

iv. Como abrazados desde sus cenizas   infinitos
   Irguiéndose con los pastos

v. Porque Chile entero se abrazaba   jubiloso   con
   las criaturas inmaculadas del firmamento

Para que todo el firmamento relumbre extendiéndose
sobre los valles y Chile salga a mirar allí el verdor que
para ellos se pidieron   esplendentes: las criaturas que
les bañaba de paz el universo

vi. Porque adorados te decían los verdes pastos de
   Chile

vii. Allí miraron esplender las llanuras   embelesados
    como volándose

viii. Entonces   como si un amor les naciera   por todo
     Chile vieron alzarse las criaturas de este vuelo   ay
     paloma   de paz por siempre sí todos los valles

COMMON IDYLL

   i. Embrace one another then the plains of this flight

   ii. That as much as is alive embrace immaculate over
        these pastures

So that Chile all blushing come out to look at herself through the
valleys and as much as is alive see then the peace they asked of
themselves: the immaculate green of these pastures

   iii. Because high they wept of happiness above the
         plains

   iv. As if embraced from their own ashes   limitless
        Lifting themselves up with the pastures

   v. Because all Chile embraced its own self   overjoyed
       with the immaculate beings of the sky

So that all heaven gleam extending itself over the valleys and
Chile come out to see there at the greenness that for their
own selves they asked   splendorous: the beings the universe
cleansed with peace

   vi. Because adored they called you the green pastures
        of Chile

   vii. There they watched the plains splendor   enraptured
         as if they themselves were high

   viii. Then   as if love were born to them   through all of
          Chile they saw the beings of this flight lift themselves
          up   oh dove of peace for always yes all the valleys

ESPLENDOR EN EL VIENTO

Inenarrables   toda la aldea
vio entonces
el esplendor en el viento

Barridos de luz   los pies de esa muchedumbre apenas
parecían rozar este suelo

Acercándose en pequeños grupos como si tras ellos
fuera el viento que los empujara   igual que hojas
tocados en la boca   hasta irrumpir en una sola voz
cantándose la sangre que dentro de ellos les latía

Pinchándose las cuencas de los ojos para saber si no
era un sueño el que los llevaba   mirando más arriba
desde donde salían a encontrarlos la muchedumbre de
sus hermanos   con los brazos abiertos   como si una
volada de luz los arrastrara cantando hacia ellos

PERO ESCUCHA SI TÚ NO PROVIENES DE UN BARRIO POBRE DE SANTIAGO
ES DIFÍCIL QUE ME ENTIENDAS TÚ NO SABRÍAS NADA DE LA VIDA QUE
LLEVAMOS MIRA ES SIN ALIENTO ES LA DEMENCIA ES HACERSE PEDAZOS
POR APENAS UN MINUTO DE FELICIDAD

SPLENDOR IN THE WIND

Unsayable   the whole village
saw then
the splendor in the wind

Swept by light   the feet of that multitude barely
seemed to stroke this ground

Drawing near in small groups as if behind them
were the wind that pushed them   just as leaves
their mouths touched until emerging in one voice
singing their own blood that pulsed within them

Pinching the hollows of their own eyes to know if it
was a dream that took them   looking further above
from where they came out to find them the multitude
of their sisters and brothers   with arms open   as if
one flight of light dragged them singing toward them

BUT LISTEN IF YOU DON'T COME FROM A POOR BARRIO IN SANTIAGO YOU WON'T
GET IT YOU DON'T KNOW A THING ABOUT WHAT WE LIVE LOOK THERE'S NO AIR IT'S
GOING   OUT   OF   YOUR   FUCKING   MIND   IT'S   BREAKING   INTO   PIECES
FOR BARELY A MINUTE OF HAPPINESS

CANTO A SU AMOR DESAPARECIDO

SONG FOR HIS DISAPPEARED LOVE

Ahora Zurita—me largó—ya que de puro verso
y desgarro pudiste entrar aquí, en nuestras
pesadillas; ¿tú puedes decirme dónde está mi hijo?

So Zurita—he came at me—now that all verse and heartbreak you made it in here, into our nightmares: can you tell me where's my son?

—A *la Paisa*

—A *las Madres de la Plaza de Mayo*

—A *la Agrupación de Familiares de los que no aparecen*

—A *todos los tortura, palomos de amor, países chilenos y asesinos*

—*For la Paisa*

—*For the mothers of the Plaza de Mayo*

—*For the Association of Family Members of the ones who can't be found*

—*For all those torture, doves of love, Chilean countries and assassins*

CANTO A SU AMOR DESAPARECIDO

Canté, canté de amor, con la cara toda bañada canté de amor y los muchachos me sonrieron. Más fuerte canté, la pasión puse, el sueño, la lágrima. Canté la canción de los viejos galpones de concreto. Unos sobre otros decenas de nichos los llenaban. En cada uno hay un país, son como niños, están muertos. Todos yacen allí, países negros, África y sudacas. Yo les canté así de amor la pena a los países. Miles de cruces llenaban hasta el fin el campo. Entera su enamorada canté así. Canté el amor:

> Fue el tormento, los golpes y en pedazos nos rompimos. Yo alcancé a oírte pero la luz se iba.
> Te busqué entre los destrozados, hablé contigo. Tus restos me miraron y yo te abracé. Todo acabó.
> No queda nada. Pero muerta te amo y nos amamos, aunque esto nadie pueda entenderlo.

—Sí, sí miles de cruces llenaban hasta el fin el campo.
—Llegué desde los sitios más lejanos, con toneladas de cerveza adentro y
—ganas de desaguar.
—Así llegué a los viejos galpones de concreto.
—De cerca eran cuarteles rectangulares, con sus vidrios rotos y olor a pichí,
—semen, sangre y moco hendían.

SONG FOR HIS DISAPPEARED LOVE

I sang, I sang about love, with my face soaked I sang about love and the boys they smiled at me. I sang harder, with passion, the dream and tears. I sang the song about the old concrete warehouses. One on top of the other dozens of niches filled them. In each there's a country, like children, they're dead. They all lay there, black countries, Africa and wetbacks. I sang like this to them about love sorrow to the countries. Thousands of crosses filled the countryside. All her enamored woman this is how I sang. I sang love:

> It was agony, the beatings and we broke into pieces. I managed to hear you but the light was fading.
> I searched for you among the ruined, I spoke with you. What was left of you saw me and I held you. It all ended.
> Nothing's left. But dead I love you and we love one another even though no one can understand.

—Yes, yes, thousands of crosses filled the countryside.
—I got here from all over the place, with a shitload of beer in me,
—dying to take a piss.
—That's how I got to the old concrete warehouses.
—Up close they were rectangle camps, with broken glass and the smell of urine,
—semen, blood, and mucus reeked.

—Vi gente desgreñada, hombres picoteados de viruela y miles de cruces en
—la nevera, oh sí, oh sí.
—Moviendo las piernas a todos esos podridos tíos invoqué.
—Todo se había borrado menos los malditos galpones.
—Rey un perverso de la cintura quiso tomarme, pero aymara el número de
—Mi guardián puse sobre el pasto y huyó.
—Después me vendaron la vista. Vi a la virgen, vi a Jesús, vi a mi madre
—Despellejándome a golpes.
—En la oscuridad te busqué, pero nada pueden ver los chicos lindos bajo la
—Venda de los ojos.
—Yo vi a la virgen, a Satán y al señor K.
—Todo estaba seco frente a los nichos de concreto.
—El teniente dijo "vamos", pero yo busco y lloré por mi muchacho.
—   Ay amor
—Maldición, dijo el teniente, vamos a colorear un poco.
—Murió mi chica. Murió mi chico. Desaparecieron todos.

Desiertos e amor.

Ay, amor, quebrados caímos y en la caída lloré mirándote. Fue golpe tras golpe, pero los últimos ya no eran necesarios. Apenas un poco nos arrastramos entre los cuerpos derrumbados para quedar juntos, para quedar uno al lado del otro. No es duro ni la soledad. Nada ha sucedido y mi sueño se levanta y cae como siempre. Como los días. Como la noche. Todo mi amor está aquí y se ha quedado:

—*Pegado a las rocas al mar y a las montañas.*
—*Pegado, pegado a las rocas al mar y a las montañas.*

—I saw messed up people, men blistered with smallpox and thousands of crosses
—in the cooler, oh yes, oh yes.
—Turning my legs for all those rot up men I begged.
—Everything had been erased except the damned warehouses.
—Ray a pervert wanted to grab me by the waist, but aymara I tried
—My guard's number out in the grass and he ran off.
—Then they blindfolded me. I saw the virgin, I saw Jesus, I saw mother
—Blows whipping off my skin.
—I looked for you in the dark, but pretty boys can't see anything beneath the
—Blindfold.
—I saw the virgin I saw Satan and Mr. K.
—Everything was dry in front of the concrete niches.
—The lieutenant said "let's go," but I am in search of and cried for my son.
—   Oh love
—Goddamn, said the lieutenant, let's color a little.
—My girl died. My boy died. They all disappeared.

Deserts of love.

Oh, love, broken we fell and as I fell I wept looking at you. It was blow after blow, but the last ones weren't necessary. We barely managed to drag ourselves among the fallen bodies to stay together, to stay one next to the other. Loneliness isn't hard, nothing has happened and my dream lifts up and falls like always. Like days. Like the night. All my love is here and here it stays:

—*Bound to the rocks the sea and the mountains.*
—*Bound, bound to the rocks the sea and the mountains.*

—Recorrí muchas partes.
—Mis amigos sollozaban dentro de los viejos galpones de concreto.
—Los muchachos aullaban.
—Vamos, hemos llegado donde nos decían—le grité a mi lindo chico.
—Goteando de la cara me acompañaban los Sres.
—Pero a nadie encontré para decirles "buenos días", sólo unos brujos con
—máuser ordenándome una bien sangrienta.
—Yo dije—están locos, ellos dijeron—no lo creas.
—Sólo las cruces se veían y los dos viejos galpones cubiertos de algo.
—De un bayonetazo me cercenaron el hombro y sentí mi brazo al caer al
—pasto.
—Y luego con él golpearon a mis amigos.
—Siguieron y siguieron pero cuando les empezaron a dar a mis padres
—corrí al urinario a vomitar.
—Inmensas praderas se formaban en cada una de las arcadas, las nubes
—rompiendo el cielo y los cerros acercándose.
—Cómo te llamas y qué haces me preguntaron.
—Mira tiene un buen cul. Cómo te llamas buen culo bastarda chica, me
—preguntaron.
—Pero mi amor ha quedado pegado en las rocas, el mar y las montañas.
—Pero mi amor te digo, ha quedad adherido en las rocas, el mar y las
—montañas.
—Ellas no conocen los malditos galpones de concreto.
—Ellas son. Yo vengo con mis amigos sollozando.
—Yo vengo de muchos lugares.
—Fumo y pongo con los chicos. Sólo un poco del viejo pone y saca.
—Es bueno para ver colores.
—Pero nos están cavando frente a las puertas.
—Pero nos están rajando, te digo.
—Oh sí lindo chico.
—Claro—dijo el guardia, hay que arrancarl el cáncer de raíz.
—Oh sí, oh, sí.
—El hombro cortado me sangraba y era olor raro la sangre.
—Dando vueltas se ven los dos enormes galpones.
—Marcas de T.N.T., guardias y gruesas alambradas cubren sus vidrios
—rotos.
—Pero a nosotros nunca nos hallarán porque nuestro amor está pegado a
—las rocas, al mar y a las montañas.
—Pegado, pegado a las rocas, al mar y a las montañas.

—I went all over.
—My friends sobbed inside the old concrete warehouses.
—The kids howled.
—Come on, we got to where they said—I yelled to my pretty boy.
—My face dripping the gentlemen came with me.
—But I couldn't find anyone to say "good morning" to, only some witches with
—a mauser ordering a real bloody one for me.
—I said—you're crazy, and they said—don't believe it.
—Only the crosses could be seen and the two old warehouses covered by something.
—From one bayonet blow they clipped my shoulder and I felt my arm as I fell
—to the grass.
—Then with it they beat my friends.
—They went on and on, but when they began to strike my parents
—I ran to the urinal to throw up.
—Immense prairies formed with each heave, the clouds
—breaking the sky and the hills coming on.
—What's your name and what do you do they asked me.
—Look he's got a tight ass. What's your name tight ass bastard bitch, they
—said.
—But my love is still bound on the rocks, the sea and the mountains.
—But my love I tell you, is still stuck on the rocks, the sea and
—mountains.
—They don't know the goddamned concrete warehouses.
—They are them. I come with my friends sobbing.
—I come from all over.
—I smoke and hook up with the guys. Just some old fashioned hook up.
—It's good for seeing colors.
—I'm telling you, they dig us out at our doors.
—I'm telling you, they rip us apart,
—Oh yes, pretty boy.
—Of course—said the guard, you have to yank the cancer from its root,
—Oh yes, oh, yes
—My sliced up shoulder bled and the blood it was foul.
—If you turn around you can see the two huge warehouses.
—Marks of TNT, guards and thick barbed wire cover its broken
—glass.
—But they won't ever find us because our love is bound to
—the rocks, to the sea and the mountains,
—Bound, bound to the rocks, to the sea and the mountains.

—Pegado, pegado a las rocas, al mar y a las montañas.
—Murió mi chica, murió mi chico, desaparecieron todos.

Desiertos de amor.

Nos descargaron cal y piedras encima. Por un segundo temí que te hicieran daño. Ay amor, cuando sentí el primer estrépito me pegué todavía un poco más a ti. Fue algo.
Sí, seguro fue algo. Sentí las piedras aplastándote y yo creí que gritarías, pero no. El amor son las cosas que pasan. Nuestro amor muerto no pasa.

Es dulce y no. Fue el último crujido y ya no hubo necesidad de moverse. Todo ahora se mueve.
Tus pupilas están fijas, pero cuatro ojos infinitamente abiertos ven más que dos. Por eso nos vimos.
Por eso nos hablamos, y con tu espinazo sostienes el mío. Y aunque nadie lo verá, yo alguna vez pensé que sería bueno esto, que está bien. Que sería.

Me derrumbé a tu lado creyendo que era yo la que me arrojaba.
El pasto estará creciendo me imagino. En verdad me gustan más las piedras creí, no, el pasto.
Creí que eras tú y era yo. Que yo aún vivía, pero al irme sobre ti algo de tu vida me desmintió. Fue sólo un segundo, porque después te doblaste tú también y el amor nos creció como los asesinatos.

Ahora todos son caídos menos nosotros los caídos.
Ahora todo el universo eres tú y yo menos tú y yo. Tras los golpes, ya idos, nos desplazamos un poco y destrozada yo fui lo único que sentiste acercarse.
Nadie sabrá el destino, porque tú eres el que busco, el que cuido. Llorona de ti tal vez seamos todos una sola cosa. Yo ahora lo sé pero no importa.

—Ay, grandes glaciares se acercan, grandes glaciares sobre los techos de
—nuestro amor.
—Eh ronca, gritó mi lindo, los dinosaurios se levantan. Los helicópteros
—bajan y bajan.

—Bound, bound to the rocks, to the sea and the mountains.
—My girl died, my boy died, they all disappeared.

Deserts of love.

They dumped lime and stones all over us. For just a second I was afraid they would hurt you.
Oh love, when I felt the first thrust I pushed up against you to get even closer. It was something.
Yes, for sure it was something. I felt the stones crushing you and I thought you would scream, but no.
Love these are things that come to an end. Our dead love doesn't end.

It's sweet and it isn't. It was the final crash and there was no more need to move. Every thing now moves.
Your pupils are still, but four eyes infinitely open see more than two.
That's why we saw each other.
That's why we speak, and with that spine of yours you hold up mine. And even though no one will see this, I sometimes thought that this would be good, that it's okay. That it would be.

I collapsed at your side thinking I was the one who threw myself down.
The grass must be growing I imagine. In truth I like stones I thought, no, the grass.
I thought it was you and it was me. That I even now was alive, but as I fell on you something of your life proved me wrong. It was just for a moment, because then you folded over too and love grew us like the assassinations.

Now all are fallen except us the fallen.
Now the whole universe is you and me without you and me.
Between the blows, already gone, we were shifted a little and wrecked I was the only one you felt move closer.
No one knows destiny, because you are the one I look for, the one I care for. Llorona for you maybe one day we'll be one same thing. I know this now but it doesn't matter.

—Oh, great glaciers close in, great glaciers ceilings over
—our love.
—Eh raspy girl, my lovely boy cried out, the dinosaurs are waking up. The helicopters
—come down and down.

—Donde yacen los viejos galpones, las paredes muy altas con torres de
—T.V.
—Tú podrías aparecer en las pantallas, oh sí amor.
—En mis sueños enciendo el dial y allí apareces en blanco y negro.
—Digo:—ése es el chico que soñaba, ése es el chico que soñaba.
—Cuando despierto sólo hay heridos en un largo patio y cueros cabelludos
—colgando de las antenas.
—Oigan amigos—les grité—esas épocas ya pasaron. Sólo se rieron de mí.
—Marcaron a los muchachos y a bayonetazos les cortaron el pelo.
—¿Fumas marihuana? ¿Aspiras neoprén? ¿Qué mierda fumas rojo asque-
—roso?
—Pero son lindos. Aun así yo me reglo de verlos, mojo la cama y fumo.
—Yo me enamoro de ellos, me regio y me pinto entera. Envuelta en
—lágrimas los saludo,
—pero todos sueñan hoy el sueño de la muerte, oh sí lindo chico.
—Grandes glaciares vienen a llevarse ahora los restos de nuestro amor.
—Grandes glaciares vienen a tragarse los nichos de nuestro amor.
—Las nicherías están una frente a la otra.
—De lejos parecen bloques.
—Todo lo vi mientras fuerte me daban pero me viré, y mi guardián no pudo
—retenerme.
—Allí conocí los colore y vi al Verdadero Dios gritando dentro de los
—helados galpones de concreto,
—aullando dentro de los fantasmas galpones de concreto,
—mojándome entera dentro de los imposibles galpones de concreto.
—Mula chilena—me insultaba mi madre—ya llegará también tu hora.
—Me viré por muchos lugares y vi a mis viejos sin salir de allí.
—Son como Dios.
—Pero ellos no saben que su cachorra se está muriendo de amor y golpes
—en los viejos galpones.
—Ahora me buscan pobres viejos ateridos.
—Preñándonos de gruesos escupitajos, juntos, jóvenes y viejos reventa-
—remos.
—   ay amor reventaremos
—   ay amor reventaremos
—La generación sudaca canta folk, baila rock, pero todos se están murien-
—do con la vista vendada en la barriga de los galpones.
—En cada nicho hay un país, están allí, son los países sudamericanos.
—Grandes glaciares vienen a recogerlos.

—Where the old warehouses are, the real high walls with TV
—Towers.
—You could end up on those screens, oh yes my love.
—In my dreams I turn the dial and there you are in black and white.
—I say:—that's the guy in my dream, it's the guy in my dream.
—When I wake there're only wounded people in a long yard and scalps
—hanging from the antennas.
—Listen friends—I yelled out—those times have passed already. They just laughed at me.
—They marked the guys and with bayonet blows cut their hair.
—You smoke pot? You sniff neoprene? What kind of shit you smoke dirty red?
—But they're lovely. With all that I go on the rag when I see them, wet my bed and smoke.
—I fall in love with them, do myself up and paint my whole face. Drenched in
—tears I say hello,
—but everyone today dreams the dream of death, oh yes pretty boy.
—Great glaciers come now to take away the remains of our love.
—Great glaciers come to swallow the niches of our love.
—The niches are one in front of the other.
—From far off they look like blocks.
—I saw everything while they were hitting me hard but I turned, and my warden couldn't
—hold me back.
—Over there I got to know colors and saw the True God yelling inside the
—freezing concrete warehouses,
—howling inside the phantom concrete warehouses,
—getting completely soaked in the not possible concrete warehouses.
—Chilean ass—my mother'd put me down—your time will come too.
—I went all over the place and saw my parents without even leaving.
—They're like God.
—But they don't know their pup is dying of love and blows
—in the old warehouses.
—Now they look for me my poor folks, scared to death.
—Knocking us up with thick spits, together, young and old we will be
—broken.
—   oh love we'll break
—   oh love we'll break
—The wetback generation sings folk, dances rock, but they're all dy-
—ing with their eyes blindfolded in the warehouse bowels.
—In each niche there's a country, they are there, they are the South American countries.
—Great glaciers come to collect them

—blancos glaciares, sí hermano, sobre los techos se acercan.

—Murió mi chica, murió mi chico, desaparecieron todos.

Desiertos de amor.

Lloré así y canté. Aullando los perros perseguían a los muchachos y los guardias sitiaban.

Lloré y más fuerte mientras los cuerpos caían. Blanco y negro lloré el canto, el canto a su amor desaparecido.

Todo el desespero lloré.

El pasto sube hasta las nicherías. Los muchachos paisa le dije ten; ten mi pena y se apaga.

Nostalgia cantamos por los países y por el país chileno.

Procesión fue y sentencia, cruzamos los otros nichos y frente al del país nuestro estalló el salmo.

Toda la pena.

Todo el salmo cayó entonces sobre su amor que no estaba.

De nostalgia cantó por ellos, por los países muertos puse no, no dolía.

Los países están muertos. Un Galpón se llama Sudamérica y el otro América del norte.

Tormento me dio la vista, dije abriéndome. El responso cantamos.

Entera mi mala estrella canté entonces el canto a mi amor que se iba. Muchas cruces se llamaban e iban.

Todos paisanos dije llorando se ha ido. Se fue, y yo no peno ni no peno.

La Internacional de los países muertos creció subiendo y mi amor puse. Todo el amor paisa, todo el lloro mío sumé y sonó entonces la General de los países muertos.

Así desangré yo la herida y al partir rojo sonó el canto a mi amor desaparecido. Todas estaban como abriéndose igual que fosas estas letritas, el grito, el país puse no, no dolía.

—Cantando, cantando a su amor desaparecido.

—Cantando, cantando a su amor desaparecido.

—Sí hermosa chica mía, lindo chico mío, es mi karma ¿no?

—Todos los países míos natales se llaman del amor mío, es mi lindo y

—caído. Oh sí, oh sí.

—Todos están allí, en los nichos flotan.

—white glaciers, yes brother, ceiling over they draw near.
—My girl died, my boy died, they all disappeared.

Deserts of love.

I wept like this and sang. Howling the dogs hunted the boys down and the guards would surround them.
I wept and harder as the bodies fell. White and black I wept the song, the song for his disappeared love.
All despair I wept.
The grass is as high as the niches. The guys paisa I said take this; have my sorrow and then it's put out.

We sing nostalgia for the countries and for the Chilean country.
Procession and judgment, we crossed the other niches and in front of our country the psalm broke out.
All sorrow.
The whole psalm fell then over our love that wasn't there. Of nostalgia she sang for them, for the dead countries I put no, that it didn't hurt.

The countries are dead. One Warehouse is called South America and the other North. Tormented by what I saw, I said opening myself up. We sing the responsorial. Entirely my ill star I sang then the song of my love that was leaving. Many crosses they were called and went. All the paisanos I said weeping he has gone. He left, and I do not grieve or grieve.

The International of the dead countries grew rising and I put my love. All my love paisa, all weeping I added and then sounded the Common of the dead countries. Like that I drained the wound and when it split red it sounded the song of my disappeared love. All were as if opening themselves up the same as pits those small letters, the scream, the country I put no, it didn't hurt.

—Singing, singing for his disappeared love.
—Singing, singing for his disappeared love.
—Yes my beautiful girl, my lovely boy, this is karma, right?
—All the countries of my birth are named by my love, it is my lindo and
—my fallen. Oh yes, oh yes.
—They are all there, they're floating in the niches.

—Todos los muchachos míos están destrozados, es mi karma ¿no?
—Me empapo mucho y te quiero todo digo.
—Cantando, oh sí, cantando a su amor desaparecido.
—Cantando, oh sí sí, cantando a su amor desaparecido.

Argentina, Uruguay y los países chilenos del amor mío y desaparecido. Por escalera se sube de un país a otro. Por ascensores se sube o por aviones del amor mío que también baja las penumbras y a veces sube. Allí andamos yo y tú. Allí andamos, entre los nichos tú y yo que hablamos:—¿Me comiste? ¿por qué tenías hambre chileno me comiste?

Te quería, te quería tanto, dice, que toda la noche negra silbó y yo te sostuve con mi mano y lo viste.
Es cosa sólo de muertos.
Sí, es sólo cosa de los muertos el ver cada una de estas letras abriéndose en nichos.
Letras, letritas, dice, tumbas del amor ido dice. Yo te sostuve con mi mano y lo viste. Países idos dice.

¿No te apenaste? Flores del Central país cambiaron y era que yo me moría. De tu lado me morí y me pusieron arriba como los países argentinos están ubicados sobre los chilenos. Todos van subiendo unos sobre otros. Nichos del galpón Sudamericano, y muertos se llaman. Nos murieron—digo—de la pena y se llaman.

Del amor desaparecido también se llaman los países. Enmurallados yacen como nosotros.
Masacraron a los chicos y los países se quedaron. Nosotros somos ellos, tiré. Fue duro.
Algunos se apodan Países del Hambre, o bien USA en el nicho americano, digo. Más atrás están los otros. Amor mío; somos nos comidos.

Fin. Y entonces:

. . . Reventada de amor toda la enamorada que quepa te cantó allí. Fue más hondo todavía; más debajo de los hoyos negros, del grito, de la pesadilla. Allí la mujer en amor te contó esta historia; es descripción, mapas y países ennichados, pero toda su enamorada te cantó allí. Corte. Tu desierto de amor. Corte. Y entonces:

—All my boys are torn apart, this is my karma, right?
—I'm soaked and I love all of you I say.
—Singing, oh yes, singing for his disappeared love.
—Singing, oh yes yes, singing for his disappeared love.

Argentina, Uruguay and Chilean countries of love that's mine and disappeared. Through stairs you walk up from one country to another. On elevators you go up or on airplanes of love that's mine that also descends the penumbras and sometimes ascends. There we went, among the niches we who spoke:—Did you eat me up? Because you Chilean were hungry did you eat me?

Didn't it break your heart? Flowers of the Central country changed and it was because I was dying. From your side I died and they put me above like the Argentine countries are found above the Chilean ones. They all go above the other. Niches of the South American warehouse, and dead they're called. They died us—I say—of sorrow and they call out to one another.

I loved you, I loved you so much, he says, that the whole black night whistled and I held you with my hand and you saw it. It's a dead people thing. Yes, it's something only the dead can do to see each of these letters open up into niches. Small letters, he says, tombs of love gone he says. I held you with my hand and you saw it. Countries gone he says.

Of disappeared love the countries also call out. Walled up they lie like us. They massacred the young and the countries were left. We are they, I cried out. It was hard. Some are labeled Countries of Hunger, or also USA in the American niche, I say. Further back are the others. My love; we are we eaten.

The end. And then:

. . . Split open of love all the enamored woman she could sang to you there. And it was even deeper; further below the black holes, the scream, the nightmare. Out there the woman in love told you this story; it is description, maps and countries in niches, but all his enamored she sang to you there. Cut. Your desert of love. Cut. And then:

111

GALPONES 12 Y 13
EN PÁRRAFOS SE LEE Y DICE:

Los focos llenaban el camino. El amor de padre y madre se lloraron todos y al abrirse las puertas subiendo recomenzó la balada. De su amor desaparecido recorrió nicho tras nicho, fosa tras fosa, buscando los ojos que no encuentra. De lápida en lápida, de lloro en lloro, por nicherías fue, por sombras fue y fue así:

WAREHOUSES 12 AND 13
IN PARAGRAPHS IT READS AND SAYS:

The floodlights filled the path. Father's love and mother's love they wept all themselves and as they opened the doors to go up the ballad began again. Of his disappeared love he ran from niche to niche, pit to pit, searching the eyes he can't find. To each lapidary weeping, it was through niches, through shadows and it was like this:

Países centrales que lloran. Murieron en fecha, época y nombre. Fueron todos habidos en Cuartel 12, en urnas que se indican y causas. Cuando crecieron en países humanos y animales interrumpieron los ríos, pero fueron todos amigos. Interrumpieron la verde selva, pero fueron amigos. Interrumpieron la pesadilla y fueron igual que los días. Sucedió en Antes. Lloraron la noche y ahora yacen. Negra es la bomba. Amén.

Nicho Arauco. Habido en Cuartel 13. Fueron extensos valles negros como los desaparecidos otros. Se anotó así: aviones sureños surcaron el cielo y luego, cuando bombardearon sus propias ciudades, brillaron por un segundo y cayeron. Quedaron todos referidos en Cuarteles con tumba escrita y advertencia. En cal borraron los restos y sólo quedó la herida final. Amén. Todos rompieron en lágrimas, Amén. Fue dura la vista. Amén.

Nicho USA. Habidos en Cuartel 12. América del Norte y remitidos a comerse entre ellos debido a sueños de cinturones espaciales, asesinatos de negros y hambre. Más abajo fueron el cielo y se llamaron Hiroshima en los países que comían; países de la Central, valles y tragadores chilenos. Todo es noche en las tumbas dicen y es la noche la tumba americana. Yace como el bisonte en Paz. Fue frase Cheyenne. Quedó escrito, Amén.

Países sudamericanos que lloran. Habidos todos por días, padecimiento y países devoradores en nichos del Cuartel 13. De arenales, ciudades indias y mundos, levantaron las masacres y no existió perdón, ni amistad ni ley. Murieron de hambre de amor en sueños que se señalan y ya nombrados. Yacen todos y descansan en paz. Por noche fosforecen y largan lamento. Está indicado procedencia y queja. Amén.

Nicho Amazonas: de la oscuridad y juego de sombras fue remitido al Cuartel que se indica con pasadizo y lugar. Fue pendencia y cruce con los países peruanos y brasileños. Del encuentro quedó la sangre, los desiertos de Sao Paulo y el cielo Amazona, quedó dicho. Quedó así dicho que fue un río de muerte y Paraguay. La sangre todavía empuja su lápida. Dice: resta y queda, Amén. No, dice fecha. No, sólo Cruz dice.

Nicho Argentina. Galpón 13, nave y nicho remitido bajo el país Perú y sobre el país Chile. De tortura en tortura, desaparecimiento y exterminio quedó hueca, como los países que se nombraron, y la noche no tuvo donde caer ni tampoco el día, Amén. País desaparecido del horror tras los cuarteles. Desde allí el viento silbó sobre la pampa inexistente y apagándose se vieron las masacradas caras, Amén. Lápida 6. Piel blanca sólo dice.

Central countries that weep. They died on a given day, period and name. They were all held in Barrack 12, in urns that are there identified and the causes. When they grew into human countries and animals they interrupted the rivers, but they were friends. They interrupted the jungle, but they were all friends. They interrupted the nightmare just like days. This happened during Before. They wept the night and now they lay. The bomb is black. Amen.

Arauco niche. Held in Barrack 13. They were long black valleys like the disappeared others. It was noted as follows: southern airplanes plowed the sky and then, when they bombarded their own cities, they shone for a second and fell. They were referred to in the Barracks with tombs written and a warning. In lime they erased the remains and the only thing left was the final wound. Amen. They all broke into tears, Amen. The sight was hard. Amen.

USA niche. Held all in Barrack 12. America of the North and sent to eat each other because of dreams they had of space belts, assassins of Blacks and hunger. Further below they were the sky and were called Hiroshima in the countries that they ate; the Central countries, the valleys and Chilean swallowers. All is night in the tombs they say and it's night the American tomb. It lays like a bison in Peace. That was a Cheyenne saying. It was written, Amen.

South American countries that weep. All of them held for days, suffering and devoured countries in niches of Barrack 13. From sands, Indian cities and worlds, they commenced the massacres and there was no pardon, no friendship or law. They died of hunger of love in dreams that are noted and already named. They all lay and rest in peace. At night they phosphoresce and let loose their lamentation. Their provenance and complaint is indicated. Amen.

Amazon niche: from the darkness and game of shadows dispatched to Barrack there indicated with passageway and place. It was conflict and strife with the Peruvian and Brazilian countries. Only blood remained from the encounter, the deserts of Sao Paulo and Amazon sky, it was said. Like this it was said that it was a river of death and Paraguay. The blood today still pushes against its tablet. It says: rest and remain, Amen. No, it says date. No, only Cross it says.

Argentine niche. Warehouse 13, ship and niche sent below the country Peru and over the country Chile. From torture to torture, disappearance and extermination, it's been left hollow, like the countries named, and night didn't have a place to fall nor day, Amen. Disappeared country of horror beyond the barracks. From there the wind whistled over the inexistent pampa and fading out you could see the massacred faces, Amen. Tablet 6. White skin it says.

Nicho del Perú y serranías. Igual que como todos referidos en Cuartel y Nave sobre los países dichos yace de Sendero Luminoso, y miseria extrema. En aviones rugieron desde el río Urubamba un camino de luz y los propios destrozados levantaron sus velas cayendo. De cholay salió el quejido: —Ay malo de mi Perú, dice, todos son tumbas. Más que en otros lloraron. Bajo el nicho Pascua yace. Fue el 7 de los vistos, se gime.

Nicho del país Central. Poco a poco la luz iba sombreando y al llegar aquí cambió de color. Fue al caer la tarde. Los países se hundieron en silencio pero debajo de sus nichos se escucharon los ríos y debajo de los ríos el grito de los negros que huían. Luego vino el sangramiento y los ríos sonaron igual que los bombarderos rugiendo. Fin. Murió Santo Domingo, ríos, montañas y verdes selvas. Se lee: fuimos buenos.

Nicho: queridos cielos el Caribe. Murieron y está consignado. Fue el último brillo intenso sobre el horizonte, el último fulgor. Miles y miles de pedazos se arrastraban pidiendo. Mancos, ciegos y comidos gritaban, luego cantaron, finalmente subieron y vieron las tumbas abrirse. Como la inmensa luna el cielo brilló otro instante más y se apagó. Fue el vacío, el paño negro del amor caribeño. En epitafio se dice, cubrió todo.

Nicho Colombia y países blancos. Anotados en conjunto. Cuartel, pasadizo y número explicado. En sierras cayeron tableteando y todo el pueblo fue la muerte primera. Luego, cuando la ciudad M-19 enrojeció el cielo, las montañas acompañaron a los caídos y entonces, de caídos y muertos, sólo una nevada fue la Colombia. Descansa en Paz; sonó así el canto de amor a la blanca. Blanco es negro. Así sea, dice, y se llora.

Nicho Paraguay. En Cuartel 13, debidamente señalizado. También masacre entre los países, guerras del Chaco, condominio y padecimiento. Yace ahora alambrado en nicho, pasadizo y tumba. Dice aquí: descanso para el guaraní Marcos, y sonó todo el Canto dice aquí, el nicho; Canto de Paz al Paraguay, canto al helicóptero abatido, al país Ipacaray que mata con la caña. Todo esto acabado. El nicho dice día y sangró.

Nicho: bosques del país El Alamo. Ardió, murieron y quedó referido sin nicho especial. En países quedaron y restos. Gigantescos aviones arrasaron tocando el lloro del amor calcinado. De láseres, guerra química y pesadilla fueron los bosques ardiendo. Fue lloro, dice, fueron quemaduras. De cenizas es la carne, quedó escrito. De carne humana son las selvas, quedó escrito. De selva son los cuerpos y calcinados, quedó así escrito.

Peru niche and mountain ranges. Just like those referenced in Barrack and Ship over said countries lies Sendero Luminoso, and extreme misery. In planes they roared from the Urubamba River a path of light and those who were themselves torn apart lifted their candles as they fell. From cholay came the wail: — Oh my wicked Peru, it says, all are graves. More than in others they wept. It lies below the Easter Island niche. Number 7 of those, it moans itself.

Niche of the Central country. Little by little light became shadow and upon arriving here it changed color. This happened at sunset. The countries sank in silence but there below the niches you could hear the rivers and there below the rivers the screams of Blacks who escaped. Then what came was the blood letting and the rivers sounded as the bombs roaring. The End. Santo Domingo died, and rivers, and mountains and green jungles. It says: we were good.

Niche: beloved skies the Caribbean. They died and this place is assigned to them. It was the last sharp blaze over the horizon, the last glow. Thousands of shattered dragged themselves begging. One-armed, blind men and eaten up they screamed, then they sang, finally they ascended and saw the tombs open up. Like the immense moon the sky blazed another instant and went out. It was the emptiness, the black cloth of Caribbean love. The epitaph reads, covered everything over.

Columbian niche and the white countries. Noted there together. Barrack, corridor and number explained. Full sierras they fell booming and the whole town was the first death. Then, when city M-19 made the sky blaze, the mountains attended to the fallen and then, of the dead with the fallen, Columbia was all snowfall. Rest in Peace; sounded the song of love to the white one. White is black. That's how it is, it says, and it cries its own self.

Niche of Paraguay. In Barrack 13, duly noted. Also a massacre between those countries, the wars of Chaco, joint lands and affliction. It lies now wired up in niche, corridor and in tomb. It says: Rest for the Guarani Marcos, and it sounded the whole Song it says here, the niche; Song of Peace for Paraguay, song for the helicopter gunned down, for the country Ipacaray that kills with reeds. All this finished. The niche says day and bled.

Niche: forests of the country El Alamo. It burned, they died and this was referenced without any special niche. In countries they were left and remains. Massive planes razed touching the weep of love scorched. Of lasers, chemical war and nightmare were the forests in flames. This was weeping, it says, they were burns. Of ashes is the flesh, it was written. Of human flesh are the jungles, it was written. Of jungle are the bodies and reduced to ashes, it was written.

Nicho: país Haití y cielo. Dice: queridos cielos de los países centrales y americanos. No fue el mismo azul se dice, porque constelado, todos rezaron mirándolo. Fueron las pavorosas naves, brujerías y bombas misiles lanzadas contra estrellas. Cuando ya terminaron, algo del azul del cielo fue el violeta, el atroz morado de los cuerpos. Ahora el azulino son los ojos que buscan. No, son negras fosas, están idos. En nicho dice: blasfemo su cielo.

Nicho: desierto del país mejicano. Bajo el país Méjico Nuevo yace. El desierto mejicano cubrió primero de arena los murales, descendió por pensamientos y al llegar a la plaza, chicanales y estudiantes levantaban sus brazos. Fue jauría y masacre, pero alcanzaron a subir unos escalones. Es como ruego y ansia el subir se dice, pero así quedó la estampa. Méjico 68 en fecha yace. Pedregal es el nicho. Dice: ni piernas ni brazos, Dios amado.

Tumba sandino y los verdes lagos. Dice Dios, dice murió Nicaragua noche amada. En nicho se anota y refiere: bombardeados por aire y mar, electrónica y sabotaje. Masacran a los muchachos en la frontera. Querido es todo el lago Nicaragua trepó encima de los volcanes y se derrumbó como el diluvio. Los caídos cubrían los campos. Todos ahora están muertos. Sandinos y países. Nicho Nicaragua se llama. Es la 17. Noche amada se lee.

Nicho: volcanes de la tierra guatemalteca. Así se llama la tumba Guatemala 14 y dice: Queridos maizales de mi país. Queridos volcanes de mi país. Queridas selvas azul de mi país, no hubo, se informa, necesidad de exterminio ni fatalidad ni asesinato. Fue muerte, campos de maíz y lava. En lengua Maya quedó la fecha y nunca se supo del fulgor de esos maizales. Nadie sabe. Como en el Perú se lloró; querido maizal, queridos cráteres. Reposa.

Nicho: país angoleño del desierto. Igual que todos los nichos descritos, igual que todos los arenales. Sobre la lápida, también en el Cuartel decía: Mi Dios es de caras oscuras. Grandes llanuras cafés ondulaban, pero no era el viento, sino los tanques y el hambre de amor lo que las movía. Pidieron, pero solamente el granate respondió y juntos todos cayeron en los arenales. Cayó el desierto Angoleño, se dice. Nicho 16. Querida arena café, decía ahora.

Tumba Nicho Venezuela. Bolívar del nicho dice. Lápidas, fosas del Tercer Mundo, como una vez se los llamó a los países. Nichos del país sudamericano, nuevo americano o todos los países que al verdor sonrieron. Adiós dicen. Todos juntos conforman el Galpón especificado. Negro fue, como las barras de las petroleras en el mar. Es el Nicho Venezuela. Allí solamente descansa un humano. Petróleo no hay ni tierra. Maldita noche.

Niche: country Haiti and sky. It says: beloved skies of the central and American countries. It wasn't the same blue, because constellated, looking upon it they all prayed. They were the terrifying ships, witchery and launched missile bombs against stars. Then when it was over, something of the blue of sky was violet, the heinous purple of those bodies. Now blue are the eyes that search. No, they're black pits, they're gone. In the niche it says: blaspheme their sky.

Niche: desert of the Mexican country. Below New Mexico it lies. The Mexican desert covered first of sand the walls, it came down through thoughts and arriving to the plaza, Chicanales and students lifted their arms. It was a pack of dogs and a massacre, but they managed to go up some steps. It says that going up was like a plea and out of fear, but that's how the engraving was left. Mexico 68 on the date it lays. The niche is a stone mound. It says: neither arms nor legs, beloved God.

Sandinista tomb and the green lakes. It says God, it says Nicaragua died beloved night. In the niche it is noted and referred to: bombarded by air and sea, electronics and sabotage. They massacred the young men at the border. Adored is all of lake Nicaragua lifted up above the volcanoes and crumbled down then like a deluge. The fallen covered over the valleys. All of them are now dead. Sandinistas and countries. Nicaragua niche it's called. It's number 17. Beloved night it reads.

Niche: volcanoes of the Guatemalan land. That's what the Guatemala tomb 14 is called and it says: Beloved maize fields of my country. Beloved volcanoes of my country. Beloved blue jungle of my country, there was no need, it informs, for extermination or fatality or assasination. It was death, maize and lava. The date was left in Maya and no one ever knew of the gleam of those maize fields. No one knows. Like Peru it wept for itself; beloved maize fields, beloved craters. Rest.

Niche: Angolan country of the desert. The same as all those niches described, same as all those sands spoken. Over the tablet, also in the same Barrack it said there: My God of dark faces. Great coffee planes undulated, but it was not the wind, but the tanks and hunger for love that moved them. They begged, but it was only the granite that responded and together they all of them fell in sands. The Angolan desert fell it says there. Niche 16. Beloved coffee sand, it said now.

Tomb Niche Venezuela. Bolivar of the niche it says. Tablets, pits of the Third World, like once that's what those countries were called. Niches of the South American country, New American or all those countries that to the greenness they smiled. Goodbye they say. All of them to the shape of the specified Warehouse. Black, like the rods of oil companies in the sea. It is the Venezuelan Niche. There only one human rests. There's no oil nor land. Damn night.

Tumba nicho Canadá y Glaciares. Albo es Dios. Sólo de blancura se vio el país Canadá; nicho del Nevado en Cuartel y pasillo; hielo de los países mandantes y de los países torturados. Fue el 19 de los vistos. Las grandes praderas muertas se elevaron como si sus pastos flotaron por última vez. Todo su amor cayó en el frío, congeló sus cacerías y el aire de las tribus quedó en el nicho blanco. Está. Dulce ha de ser la muerte en la nieve. Amén.

Tumba 21: nicho Bolivia dice; querida es toda la meseta. Indicada en Cuartel 13 y pasillo. Del amor paceño desaparecido quedó referido en lengua de aymaras un dolor tan herida la palomita y que cayó guerreando. Dice así: de derrota en derrota la más querida fue cavando esta fosa. País Bolivia se lee y se dice, capital Lechín. De noche, en sueños, paró el latido de todos estos llanos callados. Chazki larga el despido amén y chanta.

Tumba 23: país El Salvador. Nicho dice: ten piedad por tu más cercano Salvador. En galpón, tumba y epitafio quedó escrito: Nada fue tanto, nada fue tanto, nada fue tanto. Casa por casa, la que más ha tirado la sangre del hermano yace debajo de Honduras y sobre Guatemala. Cuando ya no hubo uno más explotó cantándole como a su amor el canto del desaparecido. Todos ahora duermen. Duermen y sueñan. Como la piedra, Amén.

Tumba 20: país Cuba e islas, rompientes e islas. Consignado se mira: Sierra y serranos ¿estarán? Lago y lacustres ¿estarán? Hilo e hiladoras ¿estarán? Indios y Siboneyes ¿estarán ¿Bloqueo y bloqueados ¿estarán? Puente El Mariel, La Habana y grandes rompientes ¿estarán? Leyeron todos y pararon. Desde toda la vista cayó el llanto y sonó: —murió la Isla. Sonó: —Cuba, USA y país Martí, muertos en paz, como el bisonte y el pasto.

Tumba 22: país Ecuador dice; querida es la montañosa, Amén. Cuartel y nicho también consignado. Dice: sucumbió ante hambrunas, carga de los hermanos y dominio. En lengua de shuar y quechua en padecimiento se lee: País central y selva, de pájaros colores de fuego aleteó silbando todo el lloro a su amor desaparecido. Amor del día, de la noche que en la lápida ahora dice: muertos pájaros y verdores. Selvas y nevados.

Nicho 24 de las hambrientas llanuras chilenas, argentinas, chamarritas y pampas. Son cuatro asignados en uno. Vuelta: son pedazos del país argentino que no cupieron en nicho referido. Todo el desierto de los cuarteles, Quelmes, Yaruzabi y cuarteles Tres Alamos, Baquedano y Dawson del nicho chileno. Solamente llorados en todas las tumbas cupieron, Amén. Del amor desaparecido por toda tumba, nicho y referencia, dice nada.

Niche tomb Canada and Glaciers. God is albine. Only of whiteness could the country Canada be seen; niche of the Snowed in Barrack and passageway; ice of the countries that dictate and of the tortured countries. It was 19 of the ones seen. The great dead prairies elevated as if their pastures floated for the last time. All of her love fell into the cold, froze the hunting and the tribe's air was left in the white niche. It is. It must be sweet to die in snow. Amen.

Tomb 21: Bolivia niche says; beloved is the whole plateau. Indicated in Barrack 13 and passageway. From the love of La Paz disappeared what remained is referred to in the Aymara language a sorrow so wounded the little dove and that fell warring. It says as follows: from defeat to defeat the most beloved went on digging that pit. Country Bolivia it reads, capital Lechin. At night, in dreams, the beating of all of those hushed flatlands. Chazki lets loose the leaving amen and end.

Tomb 23: country El Salvador. The niche says: have mercy on your dearest one Salvador. In warehouse, and epitaph it reads: Nothing was so much, nothing was so much, nothing was so much. House to house, the one who has most drawn blood from his brother lies below Honduras and above Guatemala. When there was not one left anymore it exploded singing to him like to her love the song of the disappeared. All now sleep. Sleep and dream. Like stone, Amen.

Tomb 20: country Cuba and islands, breakers and islands. Assigned you see: Sierra and highlanders, are they there? Lake and lacustrine, thread and spinners, are they there? Indians and Siboneyes, embargo and embargoed, are they there? El Mariel bridge, Havana and breakers, are they there? They read and stopped. From all seen the lament fell and sounded:—the Island died. It sounded:—Cuba, USA and Martí country, dead in peace, like the bison and grass.

Tomb 22: country Ecuador is noted and says; beloved is the mountainous, Amen. Barracks and niche are also identified. It says: she succumbed to famines, weight of the brothers and dominion. In these languages Shuar and Quechua in suffering it reads: Central country and green jungle, of birds colored fire flapped whistling all weeping to his disappeared love. Love of the day, love of night that on the tablet now says there: dead birds and greenness. Jungles and snowed.

Niche 24 of the hungered Chilean planes, Argentine, Chamarritas and Pampas. They are four there assigned to one. Turn: they are pieces of the Argentine country that didn't fit in the above-mentioned niche. All of the desert of the barracks, Quelmes, Yaruzabi and barracks Tres Alamos, Baquedano and Dawson of the Chilean niche. Only the wept for fit in all those tombs, Amen. From the disappeared love through all those tombs, niche and reference, it says nothing.

Nicho 25: país Uruguay; llorado del amor que no encuentra, referidos y consignados también en tortura, cacería y desaparecimiento. Tumba que va cambiando—se lee—por la pasión de los ojos que busca. Así dice. Así se lee entonces en nicho Uruguay cavado del amor ido, del amor desaparecido y término. Dice: descanso al cielo uruguayo de los ojos que busca y ahora no encuentra. Muerto entonces el charrúa, dice, no encuentra.

Tumba nicho nevado 27 de los países. Creció, creció del amor que tuvo, anota aquí la tumba. Heladas, del amor que tuve subieron las cadenas de picos nevados y fue entonces el penacho blanco que desde el oceano se ve. En Galpón y nicho están montañas y mares. El más grande es la altura de las montañas América del Sur y América del Norte. No, son cuarteles rodeados de mar, son las islas rodeadas de mar ay no. No te vas.

No te vas que es puro muero. 29 de los países. Entero fue subiendo así la oscuridad. Calamar de la noche la oscuridad que fue apresando todo y sonó allí el canto, sonó el lloro, la lluvia, de su amor toda la paisa sonó el Canto entonces, el Canto a su amor desaparecido. Me voy, run run angelito. Los países chilenos referidos y nombrados todos. Llora todavía por el hoyo que queda del amor ido. De las patrias idas ¿Me llamas tú?

Tumba Isla Pascua de los países. Nicho 26. Territorio no informa. Sólo el pájaro que recorrió fronteras y países yace. Como el tucán, así yace Pascua. De allí crecimos van diciendo, igual que la bandada, los largos valles del frente, las largas montañas del frente, las largas playas del frente. De allí nacieron van diciendo los sueños del frente; los países. Islas del amor desaparecido, dice. Todos; islas y países lloran nido y nicho.

28. Ay no te vas, gime. Tumba los Andes de los países. Me voy, larga, muere todo. Todo muere chupándose. Hubo tantas montañas como ahora son las nubes. Nubes grises, más negras y grises por el cielo encumbrándose, escalándose y desvaneciéndose. Esas son las montañas. Huecas de todos los países se largaron para abajo y fue el torrente de su amor la lluvia. Llovieron las montañas se dice la andina vidita no te vas. No te vas dice.

30. ¿Llamai tumba del amor de los países? Por duelo me llamaste? ¿Sólo por puro duelo fue? ¿Por duelo solamente fue el gran amor que lloraron tanto? Que todos tanto me iban diciendo que ya se acaba todo, que se acaba todo y fue el sueño el que se acababa. Perdiendo dice paisa te vi por pastos que se iban, paisitos dice el nicho. Perdiendo negro todo se va desaparecido por islas, países y nombres sí; ¿me llamas? ¿Me llamas tú?

Niche 25: country Uruguay; weep of the love it does not find, referred to and noted also in torture, in manhunts and disappearance. Tomb that keeps on changing—it reads—for the passion of eyes that keep on searching. That is what it says there. That is what you read there on niche Uruguay harrowed of love gone, of disappeared love and limit. It says there: rest to the Uruguayan sky of eyes that keep on searching and now do not find. The Charrua are dead then, it says, they are not found.

Tomb snow-covered niche 27 of the countries. It grew, it grew from the love it felt, notes the tomb. Ice-bound, of the love I had the chains of snowy peaks rose and then it was the white crest that can be seen from the sea. In Warehouse and niche are the mountains and seas. The largest is the height of the South American mountains and North America. No, they're the barracks surrounded by the sea, they are the islands surrounded by the sea oh no. You don't go away.

You don't go away because it's utter death. 29 of the countries. Whole the darkness like this went on rising. Squid of night the darkness seized all things and the song sounded there, the weep sounded there, the rain, for his love all hers la paisa sounded the Song then, the Song for his disappeared love. I'm leaving, run run tiny angel. The Chilean countries referred to and all of them named. Weep still for the hole that's left of the love that's gone. Of homelands gone. Is it it you? Is it you who calls me?

Easter Island tomb of the countries. Niche 26. No territory is identified. Only the bird that traversed borders and countries lies there. Like the toucan, that is how Easter Island lies. From there we grew they say, just like the flock of birds, like the valleys, like the mountains, the long beaches in front of us. From there they were born they say the dreams of what is in front of us; the countries. Easter Islands of disappeared love, it says. All; islands and countries weep nest and niche.

28. Oh don't go away, he moans. The Andes tomb of the countries. I'm leaving, he lets loose, everything dies. Everything dies sucking its own self up. There were so many mountains like there are now clouds. Gray clouds, blacker through the sky rising, ascending and vanishing. Those are the mountains. Hollow of all the countries they thrust forth down and the rain was the torrent of their love. The mountains rained they say Andina vidita you do not go away. You do not go away it says.

30. Do you call me tomb of the love of the countries? For sorrow did you call out to me? Was it all for sorrow? Was all for sorrow the great love you all wept so much? That so many times they'd tell me it ends, that all things end and really it was the dream that ended. Getting lost it says paisa I saw you through pastures that were going away, little countries the niche says. Getting lost black is every thing goes disappeared through islands, countries and names yes; do you call me? Is it you who calls?

Warehouse 12. Passageways and niche, read location by
country according to scratch and mark it says, we weep.

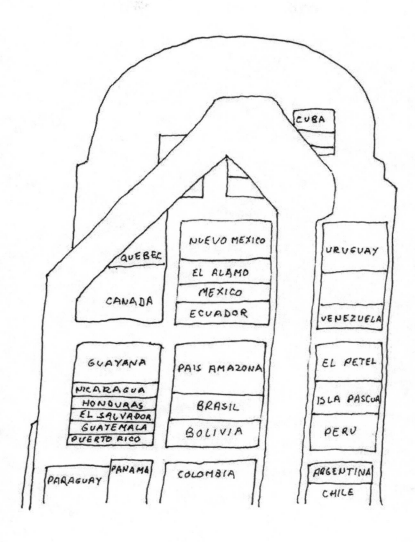

Warehouse 13. Passageways and niche, read location
according to scratch and mark oh yes it says, we weep.

CANTO DE AMOR DE LOS PAISES

¿Te acuerdas chileno del primer abandono cuando niño?

Sí, dice

¿Te acuerdas del segundo ya a los veinte y tantos?

Sí, dice

¿Sabes chileno y palomo que estamos muertos?

Sí, dice

¿Recuerdas entonces tu primer poema?

Sí, dice

sí

dice sí sí dice sí sí sí siiiiiiiiiiiiiiiiii o o o o o o o o ho hoo hooo ho
ho hoo hoooo e e e e e e e e e iiiiiii
iiiiiiiiiiiiiiiioooooooooeeeeeeiiiiiiiiiiiaaaaaaaaaaaaaaaalaaaalaaaaaaa

la   la
la

La noche canta, canta, canta, canta, canta
Ella canta, canta, canta, canta bajo la tierra

¡Aparece entonces!
levántate nueva de entre los paisitos muertos
chilenos, karatecas, somozas y traidores
levántate y lárgale de nuevo su vuelo y su canto
al que sólo por ti paisa vuela, canta y toma forma
devuélveselo a éste el más soñado y lloro
desaparecido del amor
palomo y malo

LOVE SONG OF THE COUNTRIES

Do you remember Chilean as a child the first time you were abandoned?

Yes, he says

Do you remember the second time when you were already twenty something?

Yes, he says

Do you know Chilean and dove we're dead?

Yes, he says

Do you remember then your first poem?

Yes, he says

yes

he says yes yes says yes yes yes yiiiiiiiiiiiieeeeeeeeeeeeeeeeeeeeeeeeeee
eeeeeeeeooooooooooiiiiiiiiiiiiiiiii
iiiiiiiiiiiiiiiooooooooiiiiiiiiiiiiiiieeeeeeeeeeeeeetheeeeetheeeeeeeeee

the   the

the

The night sings, sings, sings, sings, sings
She sings, sings, sings, sings below the dirt

Show yourself then!
get up then new among the little dead countries
Chileans, Karatecas, Somozas, and traitors
get up and let loose again its flight and its song
that only soars for you paisa, sings and forms
return it to this its most dreamed and wept
disappeared of love
dove and evil

Sí, dice.

Yes, he says.

DE *LA VIDA NUEVA*

FROM *NEW LIFE*

LA VIDA NUEVA

NEW LIFE

LA VIDA NUEVA

Como una vergüenza que yo tenía empecé a soñar,
mire si, soñé que estaba acurrucada contra la
pared igual que una india chamana y que una
gran cantidad de gente me rodeaba mirándome y
yo toda sola, muerta de vergüenza, trataba de
cubrirme. Iba a parir, y mi terror era qué
hacer para cortarle el cordón a la guagua cuando
ella saliera. Cada vez más encogida ya no sabía
dónde poner la vista y lo único que quería era
hacerme más chica y más chica para desaparecer
de los ojos que me observaban. Parí. Entonces
le tomé el cordón con la boca y lo corté
mordiéndolo. Creí que todo había pasado, pero
detrás venía otra pujando. Cuando ya estaba
afuera también le corté el cordón con los dientes.
Pero todavía venía una más y detrás de esa otra
y luego otra y otra y otra más, que igual parí,
una por una, rebanándoles el colgajo a
mordiscos. Entonces me fui para adentro y me
vi entera las entrañas. Me veía como por una
ventana transparente, toda por dentro me miré
y allí estaba el cordón umbilical colgando,
igual que una tripa, cortado, goteando sangre.

NEW LIFE

Like shame that possessed me I began to dream,
yes ma'am, I dreamed I was huddled against the
wall like a shaman Indian woman and that all
these people were around me just looking at me
and all alone, ashamed to death, I tried to cover
myself up. I was going to give birth, and I was
terrified of not knowing how to cut the baby's
umbilical cord when she came out. I was getting
more and more hunched over and didn't know
where to rest my eyes and I only wanted to get
smaller and smaller to disappear from the people
that watched. I gave birth. Then I grabbed the
cord with my teeth and cut biting it. I thought it
was all over, then after that one came another one
pushed. When that one was already out I also cut
the cord with my teeth. But still another one and
after that another one and then another and another
and like the others I went on giving birth, one by
one, gnawing off each flap of skin. Then I turned
inward and saw all my entrails. I saw myself
as if through a transparent window, all inside
I looked at myself and there was the umbilical
cord hanging, like tripe, cut, blood dripping.

I. LOS RÍOS ARROJADOS

I. THE RIVERS CAST DOWN

LA SÉPTIMA

Llegaron entonces los ríos: los ríos del sueño,
cielo y vientos primero, los de la vida
después. En notas empezaron a hablar entre
ellos, en silencios las cosas de la intimidad,
en pausas las del entendimiento y en acordes
todo. Así fue el encuentro, la comprensión,
el sonido. Fue mente, Opus y música su
llegada y cuando rompieron planeando sobre
las cordilleras se vio el comienzo y el acabo
al mismo tiempo.
Así es y se lee: notas de los primeros torrentes
tendieron el pasto coloreándose; miles,
millones de pastos poblando las praderas en
comunismo total de repartición, ecología, luz
y vastas planicies. Ese fue el canto de los
torrentes, el vuelo,
                        la sinfónica de las aguas.

THE SEVENTH

Then the rivers came: those rivers of the
dream, sky and winds first, those of life
came after. Among themselves they began
to speak in notes, in silence they spoke of
intimate things, in pauses of things that
pertain to understanding and all in chords.
That was the encounter, the comprehension,
the sound. Its coming was mind, Opus and
music and when they broke soaring over the
cordilleras, you could see the beginning and
end all at once.
That's how it is and how it reads: notes of the
first torrents tended the pasture coloring
themselves; thousands, millions of pastures
filling the prairies in a total communism of
repartition, ecology, light and vast planes.
That was the song of torrents, the flight,
                    the symphony of waters.

LOS RÍOS ARROJADOS

Fue el amor   ese fue el amor
Ay ese fue el amor . . .

Ay ese fue el amor que hemos llorado tanto   se
largan los ríos que se aman   arrojándose . . .

Desde el centro del cielo   lanzándose sobre las
cumbres que gritaban mirándose   Nosotros
somos los Andes que gritaron mirándose   dicen
los ríos que las llamaban   arrastrándolas

Borrascosos   tras el inmenso Pacífico que los
vientos subían   Quiénes nos subieron el dolor
de esas montañas se van diciendo las largas
praderas del cielo   Somos todos los pastos de
este mundo   les contestan partiendo los ríos
que se aman   abiertos   tirados   rompiéndose

THE RIVERS CAST DOWN

It was love   that was love
Oh that was love . . .

Oh that was the love we've wept so much   the
rivers that love one another take off   casting
themselves down . . .

From the center of the sky   rushing forth over the
cliffs that screamed seeing themselves   We are the
Andes that screamed seeing themselves   they say
the rivers that called them   dragging them off

Blustery   across the immense Pacific that the winds
brought up   Who brought up the pain of those
mountains to us they say to themselves long prairies
of the sky   We're all the pastures of this world   they
answered dividing the rivers that loved one another
open   thrown   breaking   themselves   apart

EL PRIMER PACÍFICO

Entonces, cada río cantó con
su mar, tirándose...

Como cataratas entonces   cielo abajo   parió
el mar sus aguas

Recortándose sobre la tierra que nacía al encuentro
de esas corrientes   Aquí llegamos y fue como ver
el sueño prendiendo las montañas   gritan los ríos
rayando las alturas para abajo

Lanzándose sobre las cordilleras recién nacidas que
emergían tras las demenciales líneas de las nevadas
Nacimos   les enseñamos el tono de nuestras aguas
irrumpen los arrojados ríos   como aceradas cuerdas
encadenando el primer Pacifico con las montañas

THE FIRST PACIFIC

Then, each river sang with
its sea, rushing forth . . .

Like waterfalls then   the sky below   the sea
bore its waters

Rending itself down over the earth being born to the
encounter of those currents   Here we arrived and it
was like seeing the dream taking the mountains
scream the rivers down   abrading the altitudes

Itself thrown over the just birthed cordilleras that
emerged among the demencial lines of squall   We
were born   we showed them the pitch of our waters
the hurled down rivers irrupt   like steely chords
chaining up the first Pacific with the mountains

CANTO DE LOS RÍOS QUE SE AMAN

Canto, canto de los ríos que se aman,
canto de los anchos del Biobío y las
praderas que cuando rompen cantan tras
los inmensos cielos de pasto. Canto del
cielo que se viene gritando porque todas
las cosas hablan de amor. Canta el Baker y
los ríos de las aguas más heladas que aún
no tienen nombres. Cantan sí, todas las
cosas de este mundo; las montañas y los
cielos llenos de pasto. Canto de mi amor
que eres tú, y de todas las llanuras
empapadas que se abren también cantando;
los muchachos y las muchachas abrazados
y tú que ahora caminas bajando por los
ríos: mi lluvia buena, mi verano más
ardiente, la primavera de mis sueños,

mis aguas

SONG OF THE RIVERS THAT LOVE
ONE ANOTHER

Song, song of the rivers that love one
another, song of the breadth of the
Biobio and the prairies that when
they break out sing among the
immense pasture skies. Song of the
sky that comes screaming because
all things speak of love. The Baker
sings and rivers of the most frigid
waters that still don't have names.
They sing, yes, all the things of this
world: the mountains and skies full
of grass. Song of my love who is you,
and of all the soaking plains that also
open up singing; the guys and girls
embraced and you who now walks
coming down through the rivers: my
good rain, my most ardent summer,
the spring of my dreams,

my waters

HÉCTOR GESSEL PADRE LARGA EL SEGUNDO CANTO DE LOS RÍOS

Para tocarnos llegamos
                          —Simpson

De frío   derrumbados   como pidiéndonos: así
caían los ríos

Arrastrando las ciegas cordilleras que gritan y se
aman   Es el deseo que levantó y arrasó las cumbres
cantan los torrentes   arrasándolas

Nosotras somos las ganas que se tienen contestan
las montañas   apretadas   a tientas   haciéndose
pedazos bajo las aguas   Sí: pero por qué lloramos
mirándolos insisten los ríos que vienen   rotos de
pena   tempestuosos   ahogándonos entre sus brazos

HECTOR GESSEL FATHER BEGINS THE SECOND SONG OF THE RIVERS

To touch one another we arrive
—Simpson

From   the cold   vanquished   as if asking of us:
that's how the rivers fell

Dragging the blind cordilleras that scream and love
one another   Desire is what raised and obliterated
the summits the torrents sing   obliterating them

We are what is yearned for the mountains answer
pressed together   groping   breaking apart
below the waters   Yes: but why do we weep
seeing them insist the rivers that come   undone
by sorrow   tempestuous   drowning us in their arms

II. LAS BORRADAS ESTRELLAS

II. THE STARS ERASED

JOSEFINA PESSOLO
ROMPE A LLORAR FRENTE A SU NIETO

—26 de marzo de 1986—

Peña, anima de la mia fede. Peña y roca de mi amor
nipote mío, sei bello, si bello ma cattivo. Tutto
l'amore? Todo el amor, piedra de mi pasión, pivote
mío, arco de mis estrellas. Tu abuela te habla. Tu
Veli montón de piedras a ti que te moriste. Desde
el fondo de la tierra te habla y las palabras
muertas se me agolpan en la boca per dirte, para
decirte que nadie en el mundo, que nadie te quiso
como yo. Que nadie te quiso así como yo italiana
de orionda, abuela tuya y de la tua sorella, que
nadie, que nunca nadie en el mundo los amó tanto
como yo. Ma dove ti sei perduto? ¡Yo te levanto!
¡Yo te sostengo! ¡Yo te devuelvo la fe! pero dime
dónde estás, dónde, dónde. Se vinieron los países
pero tú no estabas ni entre los nuevos ni entre
los viejos. Se vinieron miles de naves voladoras
pero no eran el brillo de tus ojos. Se vinieron
las estaciones del Nuevo Nuevo Mundo pero tú no
estabas. No estaba la noche cubriéndolo todo. No
estabas tú, mar de las estrellas. Ven ahora lindo
pequeño, ya no juegues a las escondidas conmigo.
Te moriste. Acércate ahora, cubre mi lloro y mira.

¿miro?

JOSEFINA PESSOLO
STARTS TO WEEP IN FRONT OF HER GRANDSON

—March 26, 1986—

Boulder, anima de la mia fede. Boulder and
bedrock of my love nipote mío, sei bello, si bello
ma cattivo. Tutto l'amore? My love, all of it, solid
stone of my passion, pivote mío, dome of stars.
Your abuela speaks to you. Your Veli to you
pile of stones who died. From the bottom of
earth she speaks to you and the dead words
crowd my mouth per dirte, to say to you that
no one in the world, that no one loved you as I.
That no one loved you as I Italian by birth, your
abuela and your sorella's abuela, that no one, that
no one ever in the world loved you both so much
as I. Ma dove ti sei perduto? I'll lift you up! I'll
hold you! I'll give you back your faith! But tell
me where are you, where, where. The countries
came but you were not among the new or old.
Thousands of flying ships came but they were
not the shine of your eyes. The stations of the
New New World came but you weren't there. All
things were not covered over by night. You were
not there, sea of every star. Come now lovely little
one, don't play hide and seek anymore. You died.
Come close to me now, cover my weep and look.

do I look?

III. LOS RÍOS DEL CIELO

III. THE RIVERS OF SKY

EL PACÍFICO ES EL CIELO

Torrentes entonces de la Séptima,
Quinta y Novena. Cauces de
Bach, Beethoven y Amadeus
cursos del cielo, cimas y llanuras

Estuarios y cascadas de la Cuarta
afluentes y sonidos
del aire, órganos, cumbres
del Michimahuida, Aysén y océanos:
—El Pacífico es el cielo

Torrentes de los hijos del Espolón
Yelcho, lago y aledaños:
—El cielo vivo de Chile,
espumeando

El Pacífico es el cielo   cargan entonces los ríos que se
aman   abriéndose

Como abanicos   creciendo hasta reventarse en las olas
del océano que se rompe arriba del horizonte   Son los
antiguos ríos anotan los hombres mirándolos   No: son
las mareas del cielo replican las crestas del Pacífico
álgidas   viniéndose entre las nubes

Al frente   recibiendo a los miles de ríos que una vez
salieron al encuentro de esas playas   Es el océano
repiten entrando en ellas   No: son las playas del
horizonte   es la nieve   somos nosotros subiendo
hasta encontrarnos en el torrente final de todas las
almas gritan los desollados de Chile revividos entre las
aguas   Es que soy el cielo vuelve a repetir el Pacífico
vivo   azul   espumeando de amor sobre las montañas

THE PACIFIC IS THE SKY

Torrents then of the Seventh,
Fifth, and Ninth. Riverbeds of
Bach, Beethoven, and Amadeus
rapids of the sky, peaks and pastures

Estuaries and waterfalls of the Fourth
tributaries and sounds
of air, organs, summits
of Michimahuida, Aysen, and oceans:
— The Pacific is the sky

Torrents of the sons of Espolon
Yelcho, lake, and surroundings:
— The sky of Chile alive,
spuming

The Pacific is the sky   bearing themselves then the
rivers that love each other   opening themselves

Like fans   swelling until they smash down in the waves
of the ocean that shatters over the horizon   They are the
ancient rivers note the men looking at them No: they are
the tides of the sky answer the crests of the Pacific
squalls   coming on among the clouds

In the foreground   receiving the thousands of rivers
that once went to the encounter of those beaches   It
is the ocean they repeat coming in   No: they are the
beaches of the horizon   it is the snow   it is us rising
to find each other in the final torrent of all souls
the flayed of Chile scream revived among the waters
This is because I am the sky the Pacific repeats again
alive   blue   spuming with love above the mountains

EL CRUCE DE LOS CONTINENTES

Resplandecientes, besándose las playas,
los enamorados témpanos

Y entonces   como islas rodeadas de cielo   todos los
continentes se dibujaron con su mar   arriba del aire
                                                     marchando

Cada uno al encuentro del otro   mientras los océanos
que los rodeaban resplandecían   tornasolándoles las
orillas   igual que auras   acercándose

Fundiendo de horizonte a horizonte sus besadas playas
tal como se iban fundiendo los padres con los hijos y los
hijos con toda la tierra nueva que nacía como una línea
de pasto cortándose en el cielo

Mostrando el sueño donde los hijos vuelven a palpar los
pastos de sus padres besándolos como si fueran mares
como si fueran todos los pastizales de este mundo los
que se iban elevando hasta ser el mar   Así subió el mar
de nuestro amor   de nuestras montañas y desiertos   de
nuestras playas y glaciares   nos gritan los continentes
abrazándose como se abrazan los enamorados   como se
cruzan los barcos   como se tocan los definitivos témpanos

THE CROSSING OF CONTINENTS

Resplendent, the beaches kissing one another,
the enamored icebergs

And then   like islands surrounded by sky   all the
continents drew themselves with their sea   above the
air in motion

Each one to the encounter of the other   while the oceans
surrounding them were resplendent   iridescing their
borders   just like auras   moving towards them

Merging from horizon to horizon its kissed beaches
just as parents went on merging with their children and
their children with all new earth being born like a line
of pasture splitting itself in the sky

Revealing the dream in which sons and daughters return
to palpate the parent's pastures kissing them as if they
were seas as if they were all the meadowlands of this
world those who went on elevating until being the
sea   Like that the sea rose from our love   from our
mountains and deserts from our beaches and glaciers
the continents scream to us embracing one another as
the enamored embrace   as the boats crisscross one
another   as the definitive icebergs touch one another

LOS DESAPARECIDOS LEVANTAN SUS CARAS
DESDE LOS DESIERTOS

Desde las conmovidas piedras, desde la
tierra que los miraba

De sur a norte   de este a oeste   se vieron entonces todos
los desiertos del mundo subir   incontables   como las
nebulosas   remontando los aires

Espejeando los colores del horizonte como plataformas
subiendo con el soplo del viento   ondeantes   sobre los
nuevos aires   resplandeciendo entre sus nombres

Entre el torrente de las estrellas   alumbrados   mientras
sus voladas arenas iban erigiendo las catedrales que el
sueño llamó desierto de Arizona   Atacama   pampas
del Sonora   todos arriba   como llevándonos los ojos

Mirando levantarse las nebulosas de Notre Dame   de
Pedro   de Nuestra Señora de la Asunción   de todos
los desiertos de este mundo encendidos en las alturas
Son los espejismos que los caídos de la tierra le clavaron
al horizonte   decimos nosotros admirándolas Son los
arenales de sus vidas ascendiendo en el viento nos
cantan las catedrales de los desiertos hundiéndose en el
cielo   allá   como olas que sucumben contra el océano

THE DISAPPEARED LIFT UP THEIR FACES
FROM THE DESERTS

From the stones that were moved, from the
earth that watched them

From south to north   from east to west   then all the
deserts of the world were seen rise   innumerable   like
the nebulas   mounting the airs

Reflecting the colors of the horizon like platforms rising
with the gusting wind   undulating   over the new airs
resplendescing through its names

Through the torrent of stars   enlightened   while its
soaring sands went on erecting the cathedrals that the
dream called the desert of Arizona   Atacama   pampas
of Sonora   all above   as if guiding our eyes from here

Watching lifting themselves up the nebulas of Notre
Dame   of Peter   of Our Lady of the Assumption   of
all the deserts of this world on fire in the heights   They
are the reflections that the earth's fallen have
nailed to the horizon   we say we wondering at them
They are the dunes of their lives ascending the winds the
cathedrals sing to us of the deserts plunging themselves in
the sky over there like waves that give way against the sea

DE *POEMAS MILITANTES*

FROM *MILITANT POEMS*

CANTO I

Cantemos, sí mar, un poema militante, así,
como los antiguos bardos.
Un poema que horade las aguas
igual que las aspas de esos vapores fluviales
que no hemos visto nunca.
Cantemos un poema de circunstancias
que comience en el nuevo milenio
y que no se termine.
Un poema lleno de consignas como el cielo
pero más ancho que el cielo.
Un poema que tenga nombres
impresos en millones de volantes tocándonos
hasta la luz del mar por los nuevos ojos.
Cantemos un poema del mar
saliéndosenos por los nuevos ojos.
Un poema que tenga miles y miles de banderas
te digo,
como el mar de nuevo por los ojos.

SONG I

Let's sing, yes sea, a militant poem,
like this, like the ancient bards.
A poem that slices water
just like those steamboats' blades
we've never seen.
Let's sing a poem of circumstances
that begins with the new millennium
and never ends.
A poem filled with slogans like the sky
but wider than the sky.
A poem with names
printed on millions of fliers that touch us
until the sea light is seen by new eyes.
Let's sing a poem about the sea
coming forth through new eyes.
A poem that has thousands and thousands
of flags I tell you,
like the sea once more through our eyes.

CANTO XI

A Rodrigo Marquet

Tu cara Rodrigo Marquet, la cara más hermosa
que han visto mis ojos:
pálido por supuesto, la semisonrisa,
elegantísimo, camisa verde de seda, corbata gris,
chaqueta también de seda.
Así te vistió tu hermano Teo, Pablo, para la
última pose, para mi última mirada,
                             tus ojos de flores entreabiertos.
Y yo trataba de besarte sobre el cristal y era como
si tú también trataras
y un rouge imaginario se me pegaba al vidrio
y mis lágrimas y mi saliva se iban quedando
encima, pegajosos,
igual que aguadas de nubes sobre la mirilla.
Nunca se publicaron tus poemas
y acerca de los detalles técnicos: suicidio,
accidente,
qué se sabe del último minuto.
Trataba de besarte en la boca y el rouge se me iba
quedando pegado al cristal
y era como si tú, sonriendo, abrieras tus labios
diciéndome bien está bien, besémonos.
En cuanto a si habrías estado o no en la noche de
las banderas,
tampoco son cosas fáciles de responder,
tú de bruces
sin amor en un cuarto pequeño dos meses antes.

Y sobre tus poemas: me importaban tus labios y
la dureza del vidrio,
tú sabes, todos los poetas somos amantes e inéditos.

SONG XI

For Rodrigo Marquet

Your face Rodrigo Marquet, the loveliest of faces
my eyes have seen:
pale, of course, the half-smile,
so elegant, with a green silk shirt, a gray tie,
and a coat that's silk too.
That's how your brother Teo, Pablo, dressed you
for the final pose, for the last moment I would
see you,
                              your half-closed flower eyes.
And I tried to kiss you on the glass and it was
as if also you tried
and an imaginary rouge pasted the glass
and my tears and saliva kept
on, sticking,
just as watercolor clouds over the peephole.
Your poems were never published
and as for technical details: suicide,
accident,
who knows anything about that last minute.
I was trying to kiss your mouth and the rouge
kept on pasting to the glass
and it was as if you, smiling, opened your lips
telling me okay it's okay, let's just kiss.
As far as whether or not you'd been at the night
of flags,
that's not something easy to answer either,
you facedown
in a small room and no love two months before.

And about your poems: to me your lips are what
mattered and how hard the glass,
you know, all us poets are lovers and unpublished.

DE *INRI*

FROM *INRI*

EL MAR

THE SEA

Sorprendentes carnadas llueven del cielo.
Sorprendentes carnadas sobre el mar. Abajo el
océano, arriba las inusitadas nubes de un día
claro. Sorprendentes carnadas llueven sobre el
mar. Hubo un amor que llueve, hubo un día
claro que llueve ahora sobre el mar.

Son sombras, carnadas para peces. Llueve un día
claro, un amor que no alcanzó a decirse. El amor,
ah sí el amor, llueven desde el cielo asombrosas
carnadas sobre la sombra de los peces en el mar.

Caen días claros. Extrañas carnadas pegadas de días
claros, de amores que no alcanzaron a decirles.

El mar, se dice del mar. Se dice de carnadas que
llueven y de días claros pegados a ellas, se dice de
amores inconclusos, de días claros e inconclusos
que llueven para los peces en el mar.

Strange flesh rains from the sky. Strange flesh
over the sea. Below the ocean, above the
unusual clouds on a cloudless day. Strange
flesh rains over the sea. There was a love that
rains, there was a cloudless day that now rains
over the sea.

All shadows, flesh for fish. It rains on a cloudless
day, a love that didn't get to be spoken. Love,
oh yes love, they rain from the sky astounding
flesh over the shadow of fish in the sea.

The cloudless day falls. Surprising flesh bound
to cloudless days, to loves that didn't get to tell
them.

The sea, they say of the sea. They speak of flesh
that rains and cloudless days bound to them,
they speak of unfinished loves, of cloudless and
unfinished days that rain for the fish in the sea.

Se oyen días enteros hundiéndose, se oyen
extrañas mañanas soleadas, amores inconclusos,
despedidas truncas que se hunden en el mar. Se
oyen sorprendentes carnadas que llueven pegadas
de días de sol, de amores truncos, de despedidas
que ya no. Se dice de carnadas que llueven para
los peces en el mar.

El mar azul y brillante. Se oyen cardúmenes de
peces devorando carnadas pegadas de palabras que
no, de noticias y días que no, de amores que ya no.

Se dice de cardúmenes de peces que saltan, de
torbellinos de peces que saltan.

Se oye el cielo. Se dice que llueven asombrosas
carnadas adheridas de pedazos de cielo sobre el mar.

You can hear whole days sinking, you can hear
unusual sunlit mornings, unfinished loves,
goodbyes cut short that sink in the sea. You
can hear strange flesh that rains bound
to sunlit days, to loves cut short, to goodbyes
that not anymore. They say that flesh that rains
for fish in the sea.

The blue and brilliant sea. You can hear shoals
of fish devouring flesh bound to words that no, to
news and days that no, to loves that not anymore.

They say that shoals of fish that jump, of
whirlpools of fish that jump.

You can hear the sky. They say it rains astoni-
shing flesh stuck to chunks of sky above the sea.

Oí un cielo y un mar alucinantes, oí soles
estallados de amor cayendo como frutos, oí
torbellinos de peces devorando las carnes rosa
de sorprendentes carnadas.

Oí millones de peces que son tumbas con pedazos
de cielo adentro, con cientos de palabras que no
alcanzaron a decirse, con cientos de flores de
carne roja y pedazos de cielo en los ojos. Oí
cientos de amores que quedaron fijos en un día
soleado. Llovieron carnadas desde el cielo.

Viviana llora. Viviana oyó torbellinos de peces
elevarse por el aire disputándose los bocados de
una despedida trunca, de un rezo no oído, de un
amor no dicho. Viviana está en la playa. Viviana
es hoy Chile.

El pez largo de Chile que se eleva por los aires
devorando las carnadas de sol de sus difuntos.

I heard a deranged sky and sea, I heard suns
shattered of love falling like fruit, I heard
whirlpools of fish devouring the pink meat
of strange flesh.

I heard thousands of fish tombs with chunks of sky
inside, with hundreds of words that didn't
get to be spoken, with hundreds of flowers of
red meat and chunks of sky in their eyes. I
heard hundreds of loves that remained still on
a sunlit day. Flesh rained from the sky.

Viviana cries. Viviana heard whirlpools of fish
lift themselves in the air fighting over the
mouthfuls of a goodbye cut short, of an unheard
prayer, of an unspoken love. Viviana is on the
beach. Today Viviana is Chile.

The large fish of Chile that elevates itself through
the air devouring the sun flesh of its deceased.

BRUNO SE DOBLA, CAE

BRUNO BENDS OVER, FALLS

Al frente las montañas emergen como una gasa de tul curvándose contra las sombras. La nieve de la cordillera fosforece levemente, como una gasa que flota. Arriba las infinitas estrellas y el cielo negro. Las palabras son leves, las estrellas son leves.

Escuché un campo interminable de margaritas blancas. Se doblan por el viento. Oigo el gemido de los delgados tallos al doblarse. El sonido es chirriante, agudo. Cuando el viento cesa vuelve el silencio.

Bruno. Sólo es una línea blanca que cae y se levanta. Arriba de la línea todo es negro y abajo también. Antes está la playa, lo sé, después el mar hasta el horizonte y luego el cielo. La noche es una caja cerrada negra, abajo la línea de la rompiente suena y es blanca.

Bruno era mi amigo.

In the foreground the mountains emerge like a tulle gauze undulating against the shadows. The snow on the cordillera lightly phosphoresces, like gauze that floats. Above the infinite stars and the black sky. The words are slight, the stars are slight.

I listened to a never-ending field of white daisies. They bend beneath the wind. I hear the moan of thin stems as they bend. The sound is shrieking and acute. When the wind dies down the silence returns.

Bruno. He's only a white line that falls over and gets up. Above the line everything's black and below too. In front of me is the beach, I know, then the sea up to the horizon and then sky. The night is a closed black box, below the line of the breaker sounds and is white.

Bruno was my friend.

Las ciudades pequeñas son blancas en la noche. Adelante está el mar, de él sólo se distingue la línea blanca de la espuma de la rompiente. El mar, la noche cerrada.

Escucho al conejo encandilado frente a los focos. Arriba, la gasa de la nieve de las montañas parece un tul que le fuera a caer cubriéndole la pequeña mancha de sangre que ha emergido de su pelaje pardo. Los focos iluminan otros blancos, otros pequeños pelajes con sangre.

Una pequeña mota roja de sangre cubierta con la gasa de la nieve de todas las montañas.

Susana es pequeña

At night the small cities are white. In front
is the sea, of it you can only make out the white
line of foam from the breaker. The sea, the closed
night.

I listen to the rabbit blinded by the floodlights.
Above, the gauze of mountain snow looks like
tulle that could fall on him covering the small
stain of blood that's emerged from his brown
fur. The floodlights illuminate other white,
other small furs with blood.

A small red blood speck covered with the
gauze of snow of all the mountains.

Susana is small

La tierra que cubre a Bruno es negra. La cara
de Bruno es blanca. Pero no sé si es tierra y
no sé si es agua negra o es el aire negro. La
cara de Susana también es blanca bajo el aire
o el agua o la tierra negra.

Escucho el sonido de las margaritas al doblarse.
Susana es una amiga bajo el campo negro de
margaritas blancas.

A pique el cielo negro cae sobre el mar, sobre
el campo negro, sobre la nieve como gasa de
las montañas. Arriba las estrellas se doblan
al unísono de las margaritas bajo el viento.
Las estrellas no emiten sonido alguno,
los tallos de las margaritas gritan y los oigo.

Susana dice palabras bajo el campo o el agua
o la tierra.

The dirt that covers Bruno is black. Bruno's
face is white. But I don't know if it's dirt and
I don't know if it's black water or if it's the
air that's black. Susana's face is also white
below the air or water or black dirt.

I listen to the sound of daisies as they bend.
Susana's a friend below the black field of
white daisies.

Jagged the black sky falls on the sea, on the
black field, on the snow as gauze from the
mountains. Above the stars bend over at
the same time as the daisies below the
wind. The stars don't emit any sound at
all, the daisy stems scream and I hear them.

Susana says words below the field or the
water or dirt.

Recuerdo un pasaje del mar. Sobre el horizonte el cielo tiene una diafanidad infinita y escucho el silencio que se vuelve inmenso.

Bruno era mi amigo. Susana es ahora miles de Susana. El silencio me devuelve a un camino de asfalto al lado de las montañas y al pequeño conejo encandilado inmóvil. Me detengo y regreso. En el hocico tiene una leve mota de sangre, también en el pelaje del cuello, casi no tiene peso en mis manos. Oigo el sonido de las margaritas al doblarse.

Casi no pesa. Sus incisivos suavemente enrojecidos parecen chirriarle a la luna. Susana tiene los dientes apenas rojizos. Su boca abierta le enseña los dientes apenas rojizos a la luna, como un chirrido.

En la imaginación redacto cartas devastadas de amor.

I recall a path along the sea. Over the horizon the sky has an infinite translucence and I listen to the silence that becomes immense.

Bruno was my friend. Susana is now thousands of Susana. The silence takes me back to an asphalt path beside the mountains and the small rabbit blind still. I stop and return. On its snout it has a faint blood spot, also on the fur of its neck, it doesn't weigh much in my hands. I hear the sound of the daisies when they bend.

It barely weighs anything. Its incisors softly reddened seem to be shrieking at the moon. Susana has barely reddish teeth. Her open mouth shows her barely reddish teeth to the moon, like a shriek.

I imagine I write down letters devastated by love.

Bruno está muerto, Susana está muerta. El campo negro y atrás la gasa sanguinolenta de la nieve de las montañas. La rompiente blanca sube y baja adelante. Las ciudades pequeñas son blancas en los caminos de noche. Se asemejan a copos de luz apareciendo de pronto y luego nada. Alguien los oyó y ahora son miles de caras blancas, con los dientes levemente enrojecidos y las cuencas de los ojos vacías. Mis cartas de amor. Luego nada.

Cruzo pueblos pequeños en la noche. Cruzo pelajes moteados de sangre. Ambos son leves. Bruno es leve, Susana ahora es leve.

Las palabras de amor son leves, como la noche es leve, como los tallos de las margaritas, sin embargo ellos chillan cuando el viento los dobla. Chillan y yo los escucho. Mis cartas de amor son leves. Tienen pequeñas motas de sangre y saliva.

Vuelvo a casa, dice Bruno. Susana también dice que vuelve a casa.

Bruno's dead, Susana's dead. The black
countryside and behind the bloody gauze of
mountain snow. In the foreground the white
breaker rises and falls. The small cities are white
on the paths at night. They look like luminous
flakes that appear for a moment and then nothing.
Someone heard them, and now they're thousands
of white faces, with teeth slightly reddened and the
hollows of their eyes empty. My love letters. Then
nothing.

I cross small towns at night. I cross furs mottled
with blood. Both are slight. Bruno is slight, now
Susana is slight.

Love words are slight, like the night is slight, like
the cuts in the daisies, but they screech when the
wind bends them over. They screech and I listen
to them. My love letters are slight. They have small
blood spots and saliva.

I'm going home, Bruno says. Susana says she's going
home too.

Se dobla, cae

Bruno es una pequeña garrita negra. Susana es
una pequeña garrita negra. Las margaritas se
doblan chirriando. Están las margaritas, la nieve
de gasa de las montañas. La línea de la
rompiente.

Yo lloro una patria enemiga.

Las pequeñas ciudades blancas esperan a Bruno,
las pequeñas ciudades blancas iluminadas por
focos en la noche esperan a Susana. Es día, ellos
ya no están y lloro.

He bends over, falls

Bruno is a tiny black claw. Susana's a tiny
black claw. The daisies bend over shrieking.
The daisies are there, the gauze snow of the
mountains. The breaker line.

I weep an enemy homeland.

The small white cities wait for Bruno, the
small white cities illuminated by flood-
lights at night wait for Susana. It's day,
they're gone and I weep.

EL DESCENSO

Te palpo, te toco, y las yemas de mis dedos,
habituadas a seguir siempre las tuyas, sienten
en la oscuridad que descendemos. Han cortado
todos los puentes y las cordilleras se hunden, el
Pacífico se hunde, y sus restos caen ante nosotros
como caen los restos de nuestro corazón. Frente
a la muerte alguien nos ha hablado de la
resurrección. ¿Significa eso que tus ojos vaciados
verán? ¿que mis yemas continuarán palpando las
tuyas? Mis dedos tocan en la oscuridad tus dedos
y descienden como ahora han descendido las
cumbres, el mar, como desciende nuestro amor
muerto, nuestras miradas muertas, como estas
palabras muertas. Como un campo de margaritas
que se doblan te palpo, te toco, y mis manos
buscan en la oscuridad la piel de nieve con que
quizás reviviremos. Pero no, descendidas, de las
cumbres de Los Andes sólo quedan las huellas
de estas palabras, de estas páginas muertas, de
un campo largo y muerto de flores donde las
cordilleras como mortajas blancas, con
nosotros debajo y aún abrazados, se hunden.

THE DESCENT

It is you I feel, you I touch, and my fingertips,
always used to following yours, in the
darkness feel we descend. They've cut off all
bridges and the cordilleras sink, the Pacific
sinks, and your remains fall in front of us like
the remains of our heart. Someone spoke to us
of resurrection when we faced death. Does it
mean that your hollowed eyes will see? That
the tips of my fingers will go on feeling yours?
My fingers touch in the darkness your fingers
and descend like now the summits, the sea,
have descended like our dead love, our
dead looking, like these dead words. Like a
field of daisies that bend it is you I feel,
you I touch, and my hands search in darkness
the skin of snow with which we might
live again. But no, descended, of the Andes
summits only the imprint of these words
remains, of these dead pages, of a long and dead
field of flowers where the cordilleras like black
shrouds, and us below still embraced, sink down.

DE ZURITA

FROM *ZURITA*

TU ROTA TARDE

YOUR BROKEN AFTERNOON

YOUR BROKEN AFTERNOON

CIELO ABAJO

Son los últimos minutos del atardecer del lunes 10 de septiembre de 1973 y los desfiles comenzaron hace menos de una hora. Por un momento las columnas parecieron detenerse bajo el incendiado cielo y un instante después, el estallido de las consignas y cantos inundó las calles. Al frente, interminable, el pedrerío reseco del Pacífico se alarga hasta perderse en el horizonte y sé que alguien que tal vez contuvo mis rasgos, es decir, que contuvo un insomnio, un determinado nerviosismo, una manera de hablar, reconoció entre las trituradas piedras los bordes de un puerto, Valparaíso, luego el frontis de una universidad (y pegadas a ella las imágenes rotas de una vida: una carrera de ingeniería, unos estudiantes haciendo girar sus linchacos, la enloquecedora blancura de unas rompientes cubriendo el roquerío) y, de golpe, el sonido del viento cubriendo la aridez infinita de la tierra. ¿Sucedió hace unos segundos? ¿Hace millones de años? ¿Hace apenas un día? Alzo los ojos. Inmóvil, el inmenso cielo rojo flota sobre la multitud que también se ha detenido y mira con frío, con temor, con sueño, el desahuciado atardecer.

SKY BELOW

It's the last minutes of sunset on Monday, September
10, 1973 and the processions began less than an
hour ago. For a second the lines looked like they had
stopped below the sky blazing and an instant after,
the boom of mottos and songs flooded the streets. In
the foreground, endless, pebble stones of the
Pacific extend until losing itself vanishing in the
horizon and I know that it could be that someone
who had my traits, that is, that had my insomnia,
a certain nervousness, a way of speaking, recognized
among the pulverized stones the contours of a port,
Valparaiso, then the front of a university building
(and bound to it the broken images of a life: a career
in engineering, a couple students making their
nunchucks spin, the maddening whiteness of
breakers covering the rocks) and, suddenly, the
sound of wind covering the earth's infinite aridity.
Did this happen seconds ago? Millions of years
ago? A day ? I lift my eyes. Still, the immense red
sky floats over the multitude that has also stopped
and watches cold, afraid, tired, the hopeless sunset.

CIELO ABAJO

Tengo 52 años y he llegado hasta aquí porque mi vida es vacía. La música del polaco del piso de arriba se ha vuelto cada vez más estridente y los golpeteos de sus zapatos siguiendo el ritmo resuenan en el techo acompañándome. Llevo un mes en Berlín, desde un 18 de marzo, año 2002 exactamente, en un departamento de la DAAD de paredes muy altas, desnudas y blancas, y hace un rato comencé a teclear estos recuerdos mientras afuera la primavera tarda. No sé por qué lo hago. El desierto se extiende perdiéndose en la lejanía y el cielo del atardecer se va doblando sobre él con una lentitud majestuosa, inmemorial, como si nunca hubiera sido hollado por una mirada. Abajo, las petrificadas huellas de los convoyes militares se remarcan en el lecho reseco del río, donde los restos calcinados de miles de camiones cisterna recuerdan un pasado demasiado remoto donde algo como unos seres habían vivido: mi madre Ana Canessa, mi hermana Ana María, Josefina Pessolo—Veli—la madre de mi madre, todos olvidados en la arena. Diré también mi nombre porque me desprecio y los desprecio: Raúl Zurita.

SKY BELOW

I'm 52 years old and I've gotten to this point
because my life's empty. The Pole's music from
the floor above has gotten harsher and his shoes
that pound in rhythm to the beat boom on the
ceiling keeping me company. I've been in Berlin
for a month, from 18 March 2002,
exactly, in a DAAD apartment with very high
walls, bare and white, and some time ago I started
to type out these memories while outside spring
is late. I don't know why I do this. The desert
extends itself loosing itself in the distance and
the afternoon sky folds little by little over it with
a majestic slowness, immemorial as if it had never
been tread by someone's gaze. Below, the petrified
imprints of military convoys are traced over again
in the dry riverbed, where the rusted remains of
thousands of tankers recall a past that's too
remote where something like people had lived: my
mother Ana Canessa, my sister Ana Maria, Josefina
Pessolo—Veli—my mother's mother, all forgotten
in sand. I'll also say my name because I feel
contempt for myself and them too: Raúl Zurita.

CIELO ABAJO

Conocí un botero que surcó todos los cursos de los
ríos Michimahuida, Futaleufú, Amarillo y Espolón,
sur de Chile, Amén. Él decía que tantos nombres
como la vida tienen los ríos y que por sus corrientes
se iban las almas remontando y arrepintiéndose
hasta que daban con el remanso del océano
final y Amén. Eso eran para él ese enjambre de
aguas, ahora sólo surcos de piedras en la
enormidad desnuda. En la helada, inabarcable
enormidad desnuda de un lejano planeta azuloso
girando en la noche. Abajo, proyectados en la
pantalla de un cine al aire libre un pelotón de
soldados que todavía no saben que están muertos
salen de un túnel y se reportan. Es el film *Sueños*
de Akira Kurosawa, y la que entonces era mi
pareja me toma la mano mientras llora en silencio.
Vamos remontando el torrente sin detenernos
nunca porque no hay remanso para los perdidos.
Alzo la vista desde la pantalla y veo el planeta
azuloso, el lejano montón azuloso y muerto que
gira en la congelada noche. Corte. Veré *Sueños*,
pero será infinitos años después. Ahora es el
atardecer del lunes 10 de septiembre de 1973 y la
primavera avanza como si aún fuese posible el
amor. Adelante, el océano lame los escombros
amontonados desde hace milenios sobre la playa.

SKY BELOW

I met a boatman who furrowed through all the
currents of Michimahuida, Futaleufu, Amarillo
and Espolon, south of Chile, Amen. He'd say
that rivers have as many names as life and
that through their currents souls went on
swimming upstream remorseful until reaching
backwaters of the final ocean and Amen. That
was for him that throng of waters, now just
stone furrows in the naked immensity. In the
frozen, unfathomable naked immensity of a
distant bluish planet that spun at night. Below,
projected on the screen of an open air movie
theater a platoon of soldiers that still don't
realize they're dead come out a tunnel and
report for duty. The movie is *Dreams* by Akira
Kurosawa, and the woman who was my partner
then takes my hand as I weep in silence. We
go on swimming upstream without rest because
there's no backwater for the lost. I lift my
eyes from the screen and see the bluish planet,
the distant bluish and dead heap that spins
in the frozen night. Cut. I will see *Dreams*,
but an endless number of years later. Now
it's the afternoon of Monday, September 10,
1973 and the spring is coming on as if love
were still possible. Up ahead, the ocean laps
wreckage that's piled the beach for millennia.

Han bombardeado La Moneda y se ha producido
la estampida. Las calles quedaron vacías y a esta
hora las embajadas están atestadas de gente. Yo
fui apresado en la madrugada en Valparaíso pero
eso no importa. Importa que necesito amor y estoy
solo. Tampoco importa que los tipos hayan huido
como ratas. Es la vida. Yo sé bastante de eso. O
por lo menos. A mí se me había adelantado un
poco, me refiero a la vida, claro. Tenía hijos y la
que para entonces era mi primera mujer me
buscaba. Habíamos roto hacía algunos meses,
pero igual me buscaba. Yo creo que la verdad es
siempre algo muy simple, es algo que todos
podrían entender. Los tipos corrieron a perderse y
ya está. Yo habría hecho lo mismo. Me guardaron
en la bodega de un carguero. Mal asunto. Me la
imagino perfectamente con mi estampita de
desaparecido pegada al chaleco y dando la lata.
Me refiero a la que era mi mujer, claro. Excelente
tipa, pero me la imagino perfectamente. Huyeron
como ratas. Fue lo que dije. Al primer empujón.
He comenzado a teclear esto porque estoy sólo y
necesito amor. Es simple. Todos necesitan un
poco de amor. Los boquerones de los bombardeos
han permanecido desde hace años allí. Es algo que
un niño podría entender. Quienes pasan por allí lo
hacen rápidamente. Nadie mira por mucho rato allí.

1973

They've bombarded La Moneda and a stampede
ensued. The streets are empty and now the
embassies are packed. I was arrested at dawn
in Valparaiso but that doesn't matter. What
matters is that I need love and I'm alone. It
doesn't matter that men have taken off like
rats. That's life. I know a lot about it. Or at
least as much. It had caught up with me, life,
that is. I had children and the woman who
back then was my first wife was looking for me.
We'd broken up some months before but
still she was looking for me. I think the truth
is always something very simple, it's something
everyone could understand. Men ran to hide
and there you have it. I'd have done the same
thing. They locked me up in the hold of a cargo
ship. Not good. I can see her perfectly with my
small disappeared pin stuck to her vest bitching
and moaning. I'm referring to the one who was
my wife, of course. Excellent woman, but I can
see her perfectly. They took off like rats. It's
like I said. At the first strike. I've begun to type
this because I'm alone and I need love. It's simple.
Everyone needs some love. There the gaping
maws of the bombardment remained for years.
It's something a child could understand. Those
who pass by move quickly. No one looks for long.

IN MEMORIAM
CON OTRO ATARDECER

Y eran miles de tipos
al atardecer ¿me
entiendes?
Yo no escribo cosas
bonitas ¿me entiendes?
Mamá llora y pide
perdón.
Ya pasó todo mamá.

Yo en cada letra cago
sangre ¿me entiendes?

El Pacífico es el cielo   gritaban los ahogados flotando
sobre los Andes

Mostrando las hinchadas caras que se les subían como
islas barridas por las rompientes   arriba del horizonte
espumeando

Eran los ríos No fui   No era   No estaba   anotan los
perdidos de la tierra mirando las carreteras cubrir el
lecho de los antiguos cauces   Somos los roqueríos
del cielo parecían responderles las cumbres de los
Andes sintiendo estrellarse sobre ellos las rompientes
del Pacífico   Es que soy el cielo replica el Pacífico
estruendoso   cubriendo el coágulo rojo del atardecer

IN MEMORIAM
WITH ANOTHER DUSK

And there were thousands
of guys at dusk you
understand?
I don't write pretty
things understand?
Mom cries and says
she's sorry.
It's over mama.

I shit blood in each
letter understand?

The Pacific is the sky   the drowned would scream floating
above the Andes

Showing the faces swelled that rose up like swept islands
among the breakers   spuming over the horizon

They were the rivers I was not   It was not me I wasn't
there the lost of the earth note watching roads cover over
floors of the ancient riverbeds   We are the sky's
boulders peaks of the Andes seemed to reply feeling the
breakers crash onto them   It's just that I am the sky the
Pacific responds thunderous   covering the red clot of dusk

MI NOMBRE: AKIRA KUROSAWA

Vivo desde hace tres semanas en un departamento
de la calle Storkwinkelstrasse, en el cuarto piso de
un edificio de los años 20 que se salvó de los
bombardeos y he comenzado a soñar. La laguna es
amarillenta y entre los muros de sal que la bordean
se ve el océano. La playa se llama Punta de Lobos y
las salinas están detrás. Recorremos la laguna en un
bote guiados por un remero descalzo y escucho el
sonido de las rompientes estallando a no más de 50
metros. En la dictadura el lugar se hizo conocido
porque Pinochet lo eligió como uno de sus sitios
de veraneo y hoy es un paraíso de los surfistas.
Las salinas y la laguna ya no existen y las había
olvidado por completo, pero las volví a recordar
cuando mi abuela murió: el botero remaba frente a
mí y a los lados se veían las paredes de sal. Tengo
cinco años, mi hermana tres y estamos con mi
abuela. Había nacido en Italia, en Rapallo, y llegó a
Chile con mi madre todavía niña. Ambas quedaron
viudas con dos días de diferencia. Primero mi
madre, luego mi abuela. Fue un veraneo corto. Mi
abuela murió en 1986. Yo sobreviví a una dictadura,
pero no a la vergüenza. Años después, cuando me
llegó a mí el turno, su cara se me vino encima como
una montaña blanca de sal. Quise escribirlo, pero
las palabras, como vísceras humeantes, llegaron
muertas a mis dedos. Mi nombre: Akira Kurosawa.

MY NAME: AKIRA KUROSAWA

I've been living for three weeks now in an apartment
on Storkwinkelstrasse, on the fourth floor of a building
from the 1920s that was spared bombardment and I've
begun to dream. The lagoon is yellowish and within
the massive salt walls that encircle it you can see the
ocean. The beach is called Punta de Lobos and the salt
mines are nearby. We cross the lagoon in a boat led
by a barefooted oarsman and I hear the clamor of the
breakers crashing not more than 50 meters away.
During the dictatorship the place became popular
because Pinochet turned it into his summer resort
and now it's a surfer's paradise. Neither the mines
nor the lagoon exist anymore and I'd forgotten them
completely, but I remembered them again when my
grandmother died: the boatman rowed in front of me
and beside us you could see the salt walls. I'm five years
old, my sister is three and we're with my grandmother.
Born in Italy, in Rapallo, she arrived to Chile with my
mother still a child. Both were widowed two days apart.
First my mother, then my grandmother. It was a short
summer holiday. In 1986 my grandmother died. I
survived a dictatorship, but not the shame. Many
years later, when it was my turn, her face came
down upon me like a white mountain of salt. I wanted
to write it, but the words, like smoldering entrails,
arrived dead to my fingers. My name: Akira Kurosawa.

MARGARITAS EN EL MAR

Infinitos puntos de luz brillan cerrándose en el mar
y siento que podría largarme a llorar como una
niñita. Abro los ojos y es la mierda. No tengo la
menor idea con quien terminé acostado ni pienso
en averiguarlo. En todo caso el olor no es para
hacerse ilusiones; el vómito se ha endurecido y
sus costrones me cruzan la cara y las costillas. Me
saco de encima una pierna laxa y me levanto. La
pierna parece muerta, pero no su dueño o dueña
porque se ríe dormido como si estuviera soñando
con algo muy divertido. Por los vidrios rotos de la
ventana se ve un amanecer o atardecer, da igual
Busco mis zapatos y me tropiezo con tipos
durmiendo en el suelo. No los encuentro y se los
saco a uno. Mientras se los tironeo veo el vómito
que le borra la boca y que sigue en el cuello de
otro. Son unos zapatos deformes, como si fueran
de alguien muy gordo. Me los pongo y salgo.
Los había abandonado a todos y no tengo idea
dónde ir. Al frente, mi hijo de dos años se va
hundiendo en el mar y los infinitos puntos de
luz de las olas se cierran encima de él como si
fueran minúsculas flores blancas. Los zapatos
me quedan enormes y se me salen con cada
paso. Siento que no podré contenerme y aprieto
los párpados con fuerza. Kurosawa, le digo
entonces, infinidades de margaritas cubren el mar.

DAISIES IN THE SEA

Endless points of light glimmer closing themselves
in the sea and I feel I could let loose and cry like a
little girl. I open my eyes and everything's all
fucked up. I don't have a clue who I ended up with
and don't bother finding out. In any case the smell
doesn't make me hopeful; the vomit has hardened
and the crusted chunks cross over my face and ribs.
I lift this heavy leg off me and get up. The leg is
lifeless, but not the person because he or she laughs
asleep as if dreaming about something very funny.
Through the broken glass of the window you can
see a dusk or dawn, it makes no difference. I look
for my shoes and trip over some guys asleep on the
floor. I can't find my own and take a pair off one
of them. As I pull at the shoes I see the vomit that
erases his lips and then goes down someone
else's neck. The shoes are warped, as if they
were some fat guy's. I put them on and leave. I
had left everyone behind and have no idea where
to go. In the foreground, my two-year-old son
drowns in the sea and the endless points of light
of waves close in on him as if they were small
white flowers. The shoes are huge on me and slide
off with each step. I think I can't hold it in anymore
and shut my eyelids real hard. Kurosawa, I say to
him then, an infinite number of daisies swathe the sea.

SUEÑO 210 / A KUROSAWA

Como inmensas pirámides de vidrio las montañas se
tendían transparentándose mientras el campo
intensamente rojo que llegaba hasta sus faldeos tenía
la consistencia dudosa de la sangre o del atardecer. Me
di cuenta de que me había quedado dormido mientras
escribía el guión -me ganaba la vida en eso- y que la
imagen no era seguramente más que una entre las
millones que se suceden en esos cabeceos casi
instantáneos. La pantalla del computador se había ido a
negro y al intentar mover el mouse para reanudar el
trabajo advertí que últimamente los temblores de mi
lado derecho habían recrudecido y que los dedos se
negaban a obedecerme. Nevaba. La deslumbrante
blancura hería mis ojos y el frío hacía que caminara con
torpeza, con pasos muy cortos. Recordaba haber estado
en mi infancia en ese mismo lugar y que la nieve me
había cegado mientras los otros niños me llamaban
para que los alcanzara. De pronto me sorprendió que
nevara en primavera. Al abrir los ojos vi las montañas
transparentes y más acá, infinidades de flores rojas
emergiendo de la nieve como si fueran vísceras
sangrantes. Mis dedos corrían deslizándose por el
teclado. Entendí tus películas, alcancé todavía a gritarle
a Kurosawa, entendí tus guiones: hay nieve, hay un
hombre con Parkinson que acaba de caer sobre la nieve.

DREAM 211 / FOR KUROSAWA

Like immense glass pyramids mountains hung
becoming transparent as the intensely red
countryside that reached the base of the slope
had the uncertain consistency of blood or dusk.
I realized that I'd fallen asleep while writing the
script—that's how I earned a living—and that
the image was surely not more than one among
millions that happen at those almost instantaneous
moments of nodding off. The computer screen
had gone black and as I tried to move the mouse
to begin working again, I noticed that lately the
tremors on my right side had worsened and that
my fingers wouldn't comply. It snowed. The
blinding whiteness stung my eyes and the cold
made me walk awkwardly, with very short steps.
I remembered having been in that same place
during my childhood and that the snow had blinded
me while other children would call out for me to
catch up to them. Suddenly it surprised me that it
snowed in spring. As I opened my eyes I saw
the transparent mountains and closer yet, endless
red flowers emerging from the snow as if they
were bloody entrails. My fingers ran letting
themselves go on the keyboard. I understood your
movies, I still managed to cry out to Kurosawa, I
understood your scripts: there's snow, there's
a man with Parkinson's that just fell in the snow.

SUEÑO 212 / A KUROSAWA

Papá ha vuelto

La cumbre de la montaña se alejaba perdiéndose
cielo adentro y definitivamente supe que papá iba
a morir. Recordé que hacía mucho tiempo que no
nevaba sobre Santiago y me dije que yo ya había
vivido lo suficiente, que ya era mucho mayor que
él y que estaba bien. Le agradecí que hubiese
vuelto a esperar 50 años porque yo a los 52 podía
entenderlo. Le escogí la ropa y empecé a vestirlo.
Mis camisas le quedaban algo grandes y al levantarle
la cabeza para ponerle la que me pareció mejor,
sentí el primer golpe de las lágrimas detrás de los
párpados pugnando por salir. Me volví a decir que
papá murió el 16 de febrero de 1952, a los 31 años
exactamente, y que debe haberme hecho falta, pero
no es algo en lo que hubiese pensado mucho. No
supe en qué instante regresó. Se instaló en mi pieza y
durante los últimos años alcanzamos a hablar algo.
Ahora se había muerto y yo lo vestía mientras mi
madre y mi hermana esperaban en el living. Al abrir
la puerta para avisarles que ya podían entrar, la
furia del viento y del granizo me azotó aturdiéndome
y ciego corrí a campo traviesa. Kurosawa, le grité
entonces, el volvió para morirse de nuevo conmigo.
Cuando abrí los ojos vi encima mío la blancura
delirante de la cumbre y muy abajo las primeras luces
de la ciudad encendiéndose. Sólo entonces pude llorar.

DREAM 213 / FOR KUROSAWA

Papa has returned

The mountain summit retreated vanishing the
sky within and I knew without a doubt that papa
would die. I remembered that for some time it
hadn't snowed in Santiago and I told myself I'd
already lived enough, that already I was much
older than he and that I was fine. I thanked him for
having waited 50 years to come back because at
52 I could understand him. I picked out his clothes
and began to dress him. My shirts were a little big
for him and as I lifted his head to put on the one
that seemed best I felt the first jolt of tears behind
my eyelids struggling to get out. I told myself again
that papa died the 16th of February, 1952, at exactly
31 years of age, and that I must have missed him, but
it's not something I would've thought much about. I
didn't know exactly when he came back. He moved
into my room and for the last years we've been able
to speak some. Now he had died and I dressed him
while my mother and sister waited in the living room.
As I opened the door to tell them they could come in
the fury of the wind and hail thrashed me stunning
me and blind I ran across the field. Kurosawa, I
cried out then, he returned to die again with me. As I
opened my eyes above me I saw the dizzying white
of the summit and much further below the first
lights of the city illuminating. Only then could I cry.

SUEÑO 214 / A KUROSAWA

Los farellones recortaban abajo la herradura del
mar y en lugar de las casas playeras edificadas en
las terrazas de los acantilados, se erguían arcos y
columnatas de una antigüedad indescifrable que
descendían escalonadamente hasta el comienzo
de la playa. El sol todavía alto le imprimía al mar
una solidez radiante y cuando finalmente llegué
a su orilla, la intensidad de sus tonos se abrió de
golpe inundándome los ojos. Las rompientes se
hacían cada vez más altas, más resplandecientes
y luminosas, y sin emitir un sonido sus resacas
iban y venían cubriendo la arena con infinitas
líneas de colores. Hundí entonces mis pies en los
bordes y vi que el mar eran llanuras y llanuras de
cuerpos muertos, extensiones interminables de
torsos exánimes, de vientres que ondeaban igual
que paños extendiéndose hasta el horizonte,
mientras más acá, siguiendo la curvatura de las
rompientes, los cadáveres ascendían doblándose
hasta aparecer por un segundo transparentados
en la cumbre de la ola para luego derrumbarse.
Eran millones de millones de caras con las bocas
abiertas, infinidades de espaldas, de brazos y
piernas barriendo una y otra vez la playa como
si fueran cuerdas pintadas. Kurosawa, alcancé
aún a gritarle, este no es un sueño, este es el mar.

DREAM 215 / FOR KUROSAWA

Below the bluffs sliced into the horseshoe bend
of the sea and instead of beach houses built upon
cliff terraces, rising arches and columns of an
indecipherable antiquity descended step by step
down to where the beach begins. Still high, the
sun imprinted a solid radiance upon the sea and
when I finally arrived to its edge, the tonal
intensity opened up suddenly flooding my
eyes. The breakers steadily rising, becoming
more brilliant and luminous, and without a sound
its undertows came and went covering the sand
with infinite lines of color. Then I plunged in
and saw that the sea was endless plains of
torsos and backs exhumed, of stomachs that
waved like rags extending themselves to the
horizon, while further over here, following the
curvature of the breakers, the cadavers rose
folding themselves until appearing for a
second becoming transparent at the peak of the
wave to then break apart. They were millions
of millions of faces with their mouths open,
infinite hips, arms and legs sweeping again and
again the beach as if painted ropes. Kurosawa, I
managed to cry out, this isn't a dream, this is the sea.

TU ROTA NOCHE

YOUR BROKEN NIGHT

¿DESPERTAREMOS ENTONCES?

Kjarkas palomitay mi señorita las penas de la
noche. Difuntos soldados de pasto te buscan
charangueando entre las sombras y es todo el
lloro la pena mi corazón. Corte. Mi corazón
cajita que toco para acompañarte a llorar mi
corazón. Y es mi corazón tocándote viditay
a llorar mi corazón. Corte. Las últimas
praderas se incendian y la abovedada noche
americana flota en un cielo amarillo. ¿Estarás
allí cuando despierte?
Cae la noche de pasto. A mi palomitay, a mi
palomitay se la han robado cuatro coraceros
y son las estrellas que cantan quemándose
en la noche. ¿Te rescatarán palomitay los
rifleros? ¿Los fusilados rifleros de la noche?
¿de la noche ardiendo? Corte. ¿Despertaré?
¿Despertarás? ¿Despertaremos entonces?

THEN WILL WE WAKE?

Kjarkas palomitay mi señorita the sorrows
of night. Perished grass soldiers look for
you charangueando among the shadows
and it's all lament the sorrow my soul.
Cut. Little box I touch my soul to be
with you to grieve my soul. And it's my
soul that touches you viditay to weep my
soul. Cut. The last fields were set on fire
and the vaulted American night floats in
a yellow sky. Will you be there when I
wake up?
The pasture night falls. Four cuirassiers
have taken my palomitay, my palomitay
and they are the stars that sing
burning themselves in the night. Will
the riflemen rescue you palomitay?
The gunned down riflemen of night?
Of the blazing night? Cut. Will I wake up?
Will you wake up? Then will we wake?

PRISIÓN ESTADIO CHILE

No era ése nuestro país, gritaban
nuestras sombras pasando entre
las aguas abiertas del Pacífico

Son las viejas prisiones chilenas nos gritábamos mirando
el país de tablas que emergía atravesado   cortando de lado
a lado el paso entre los espumeantes murallones del
Pacífico   largo   entero clavado   alzándose ante nosotros

    Y *el mar dejó de ser el mar y el cielo el cielo*

    Y *las cumbres eran las puntas de las tablas*

    Y *las llanuras soplaban colándose entre los*
    listones y el viento no era el viento ni el aire
    el aire

Donde de todo lo que fue ahora eran sólo entarugados
paisajes clavados unos con otros como aserruchadas
montañas mostrando arriba las empalizadas del cielo

    Y *nuestras mejillas parecían el caído cielo de*
    esas empalizadas

    Así se nos derrumbó el horizonte y los paisajes
    se llenaban de escombros en estos tabiques

    Donde hasta las rajadas aguas gritaron mirando
    los desmoronados escombros de esas vistas

Cuando entramos por el corredor de las abiertas aguas y
arrastrándonos vimos los cuarteles de tablas atravesados
entre los dos paredones del Pacífico y sobre él las gradas
rotas del estadio Chile blanqueándose bajo la nieve como
una gigantesca cordillera de palo aprisionando el horizonte

ESTADIO CHILE PRISON

That was not our country,
screamed our shadows as they passed
between the open waters of the Pacific

They're the old Chilean prisons we screamed to one another
looking at the emerging country of boards that traversed
splitting from one side to the other the path between the
spuming walls of the Pacific   long   entirely nailed
lifting itself up before us

> *And the sea was no more the sea and the*
> *sky the sky*

> *And the peaks were the boards' points*

> *And the plains blew passing through the*
> *laths and the wind wasn't the wind or the air*
> *the air*

> Where of all that was now is only wood block floor
> landscapes nailed one against the other like sawed
> off mountains showing above the sky palisades

> *And our cheeks looked like the fallen sky of those*
> *palisades*

> *Like that the horizon came down on us and the*
> *landscapes filled with the wreckage of these partitions*

> *Where even the rent waters screamed seeing the*
> *crumbled wreckage of those sights*

When we went in to the corridor of open waters and dragging
ourselves we saw the board quarters traversed among the
two massive walls of the Pacific and above it the broken
benches of the Chilean stadium whitening below the snow
like an enormous cordillera of rods imprisoning the horizon

PRISIÓN VILLA GRIMALDI

—Barracas—

Nadie es la patria, parecían
gritar las ciegas tablas
en la patria muerta del mar

Y así iban emergiendo las cárceles chilenas   las nevadas
cumbres de los Andes eran solo unas tablas clavadas en
esas barracas

En medio del abismo del océano   como si quisieran con
sus trizaduras recordarnos el infinito dolor de los campos
los cuarteles   los infinitos galpones donde nos mataron

Cuando el Pacífico se abrió y cargándonos unos a otros
vimos las estacas de una cordillera y después un cielo
muerto hundiéndose en el tajo del mar hasta ser el
silencio final que cubre nuestros despojos   todavía
clavados   todavía rotos   con los ojos todavía abiertos
mirando desde esas barracas la mirada muerta del océano

VILLA GRIMALDI PRISON

—Sheds—

No one is our homeland, the
blind boards seemed to scream
in the dead homeland of the sea

And that's how the Chilean jails began emerging   the
snowfallen peaks of the Andes were only some nailed
boards in those sheds

In the middle of the ocean abyss   as if they wanted with
their shatterings to remind us of the endless pain of the fields
the barracks   the endless warehouses where they killed us

When the Pacific opened up and bearing each other
we saw the stakes of one of the cordilleras and after
that a dead sky sinking into the slash of the sea until
being the definitive silence that covers our remains
still   nailed down   still broken   with our eyes still
open seeing from those sheds the ocean's dead gaze

Y AÚN NO AMANECE

Aún no amanece y yo tomé
tu brazo yermo y lo abracé
a mi cuello como si fueras
tú y no yo atrayéndome
a tu boca
y nuestras caras tan juntas
y tus obscenidades
ronroneadas a baja voz como
las olas de un mar calmo
donde nunca ni nadie se acaba

AND STILL NO DAWN

Still no dawn and I took
your lifeless arm and
put it around my neck
as if it were you and
not me drawing me
to your mouth
and our faces so together
and your obscenities
whispered hushed like
waves of a calm sea
where never and no one ends

TU ROTO AMANECER

YOUR BROKEN DAWN

AUSCHWITZ

Era una linda mañana de sol en Auschwitz y tú
me dijiste "no puedo creer que esté acá con el
chico de mis sueños, pellízcame para saber que
es verdad, sí hazlo, amor."
Se veía el crematorio con su enorme chimenea y
te respondí "son nuestros últimos minutos" y tú
dijiste "es tan bello morir con quien se ama, oh
sí que lo es, amor."
Más acá la estación tenía un aire funerario y en
informaciones me dijeron que podíamos pagar
la entrada con tarjeta de crédito.
Maldita economía—le dije a mi chica estoy en
blanco.
El viento comenzó a encarnizarse con nuestras
cenizas y flotamos sobre una casa de ladrillos
rojos. Nacimos en América.

Cordilleras invisibles cubrían ahora el definitivo
amanecer.

AUSCHWITZ

It was a lovely bright morning in Auschwitz and
you said "I can't believe I'm here with my dream
guy, pinch me so I know it's true, go ahead,
my love."
The crematorium and its huge chimney was visible
and I replied, "These are our last moments" and
you said "It's so beautiful to die with the one you
love, oh yes it is, my love."
Further over here the station had a funereal air
and at the information booth they told me we
could pay the entry fee with a credit card.
Goddamn economy—I said to my girlfriend I'm
broke.
The wind began to flesh itself with our ashes and
we floated over a red brick house. We were born
in America.

Invisible cordilleras now covered over the last
dawn.

AUSCHWITZ

El tren a los campos se bamboleaba de lo lindo
y por las rendijas del vagón se alcanzaban a ver
países quemados y nubes de cenizas alejándose
en el viento.
Le pregunté a mi chica si no le encontraba un
aire familiar y ella respondió "oh sí, nuestras
cenizas se mezclarán como en los puentes de
Madison, y será tan bello amor."
El portero me dijo: usted está en problemas. Me
dirigí entonces a los del vagón y les pregunté:
¿tengo problemas yo? ¿es que tengo acaso la
cara de un tipo que tiene problemas?
Paramos frente a una vieja usina y nos sacamos
la ropa. Luego cubrimos con nuestros cuerpos
una ciudad arrasada.
El tren llegó a Auschwitz al amanecer. Un río
de cenizas cruzaba ahora los puentes.

Ganas o pierdes, le dije a mi chica, esas son las
reglas acá en América.

AUSCHWITZ

The train wobbled along the tracks to the camps
and through cracks in the wagon you could see
burned landscapes and ash clouds moving further
away through the wind.
I asked my girlfriend if there wasn't a familiar air
about it and she replied, "Oh yes, our ashes will
come together like in *The Bridges of Madison
County*, and it'll be so beautiful my love."
The porter said to me: You've got a problem. So I
looked at the people in the wagon and said:
Do I have a problem? Do I in any way look like a
guy with a problem?
We stopped in front of an old factory and took
off our clothes. With our bodies then we covered
a razed city.
The train arrived to Auschwitz at dawn. The bridges
now crossed over a river of ashes.

You win you lose, I said to my girlfriend, that's how
it goes here in America.

AUSCHWITZ

Auschwitz, gritó el inspector haciendo sonar el
silbato. Afuera hacía un frío de pelarse y mi
chica me preguntaba.
A la salida había un puesto de hot dogs llamado
"Perro Judío," tiendas de jabones y largas filas
esperando su turno.
La cámara de gasas era una casa con duchas y
paredes pintadas de color frambuesa. Love,
exclamó mi chica mirándola: ¡Pero si es el
dormitorio de mamá!
La cama estaba ya deshecha e hicimos el amor
frente a los ángeles de la muerte con rapidez y
furia.
Después entramos a la sección "Crematorios."
Todavía alcanzaste a decirme
            "Love is a many splendored thing."

AUSCHWITZ

Auschwitz, the inspector shouted pulling the
whistle. It was freezing outside and my
girlfriend was asking around for me.
At the exit there was a hot dog stand called
"Jew Dog," soap shops and long lines waiting
their turn.
The gas chamber was a house with showers
and walls painted raspberry. Love, my
girlfriend blurted out looking in at it. It's
mom's room! The bed was already undone
and in front of the angels of death we made
love with haste and fury.
We went then into the "Crematoria" section.
You managed to say to me still
       "Love is a many splendored thing."

PAULINA WENDT

Un hombre que agoniza te ha soñado, un hombre
que agoniza te ha seguido. Uno que quiso morir
contigo cuando tú quisiste morir.
Allí está mi cuerpo estrellado contra los arrecifes
cuando ahogándome te vi emerger y eternamente
cerca y eternamente lejos eras tú la inalcanzable
playa.
Todo en ti es doloroso.
Te saludo entonces y saludo a lo eterno que vive
en la derrota, a lo irremediablemente destruido,
al infinito que se levanta desde los naufragios,
porque si agua fueron nuestras vidas, piedras
fueron las desgracias.
No soy yo, son mis patrias las que te hablan: el
sonido de océano que describo, las estrellas de
la recortada noche.
Iluminada de la noche tu cara sube cubriendo
el amanecer. Abres los párpados, entre ellos
millones de hombres dejan el sueño, toman sus
autobuses, salen,
                      las ciudades de agua en tus ojos

PAULINA WENDT

A man in agony has dreamed of you, a man in
agony has followed you. One that wanted to die
with you when you wanted to die.
My body is over there thrashed against the reefs
when drowning I saw you emerge and forever
close and forever far you were the unreachable
shore.
Everything in you is painful.
Then I greet you and I greet the eternal that lives
in defeat, the irredeemably destroyed,
the endless that lifts itself up from the wrecks,
because if water were our lives, stones were the
misfortunes.
It's not me, my homelands speak to you:
the ocean sound I describe, the stars from the
night cut short.
Illuminance of night your face rises covering the
dawn. You open your eyelids, among them
millions of men leave sleep behind, get on their
buses, and go out,
                    the cities of water in your eyes

PAULINA WENDT

Todo en ti está vivo y está muerto: el fulgor del
pasto en la aurora y el hilo de voz creciendo en
el diluvio, el feroz amanecer y la mansedumbre,
el grito y la piedra.
Todo mi sueño se levanta desde las piedras y te
mira.
Toda mi sed te mira, el hambre, el ansia infinita
de mi corazón.
Te miro también en el viento. En las nieves de
la cordillera sudamericana.
Allí está la calle en que esperé que amanecieras,
la noche póstuma, el país muerto en el que no
morimos. Allí están todas las heridas y golpes
cuando emergiendo del destrozado sueño volví
hacia ti los ojos y vi las desmesuradas estrellas
flotando en el cielo.
Tu cara ahora flota en el cielo, detrás corre un
río. Hay un hombre muy viejo.
Hay un hombre muy viejo en el medio del río
y tú lo miras
                    las ciudades de agua en tu ojos

PAULINA WENDT

All of you is alive and dead: the grass' gleam at
sunrise and the voice thread that grows in the
deluge, the savage dawn and docility, the scream
and stone.
All my dream gets up from the stones and looks at
you.
All my thirst looks at you, the hunger, my heart's
endless dread.
I look at you also in the wind. In the snows of the
South American cordillera.
Over there is the sky where I waited for you to
wake up, the posthumous night, the dead country
where we did not die. Over there all wounds and
beatings as I emerged from the demolished dream
I turned my eyes back toward you and saw the vast
stars floating in the sky.
Your face now floats in the sky, behind it a river.
There's such an old man.
There's such an old man in the midst of that river and
you look at him
                           the cities of water in your eyes

PAULINA WENDT

Sabes que estás muerta para el amor y no amas.
Todos los puentes están rotos y tus padres ya
cansados se devuelven sobre sus pasos, ya no
vendrán a visitarte.
Han pasado miles de años de todo eso y ahora
acabas de despertar.
Somnolienta te tocas la cara y palpas bajo la piel
el trabajo de la calavera que te sobrevivirá como
en el fondo del lago la piedra sobrevive al cuello
a la que fue atada.
Sabes que estás muerta para el amor y no amas.
Te preparas entonces un café y enciendes con
distracción la radio, te sientas, te levantas de
nuevo, abres la ducha como un cotidiano rezo
matutino y sientes el antiguo golpe.
Como hace miles de años todos los puentes han
sido arrancados y no hay salida:
Sabes que estás muerta para el amor.
Sabes que estás muerta para el amor, pero él te
ama. Levantas la cara,
                    las ciudades de agua en tus ojos

PAULINA WENDT

You know you're dead for love and don't love.
All the bridges are broken and your weary
parents go back to where they came from, they
won't return any more to visit.
They've spent a thousand years on all that and
just now you wake. Lethargic you touch your
face and feel below your skin the work of a
skeleton that will outlive you like the rock at
the lake bottom that outlives the neck it
tethered.
You know you're dead for love and don't love.
You then make yourself a cup of coffee and
distracted turn on the radio, you sit, and get
up again, turn on the shower like a daily
morning prayer and feel the old blow.
Like thousands of years ago all the bridges
had been dug out and there's no way to
leave:
You know you're dead for love.
You know you're dead for love, but he loves you.
You lift up your face,
                          the cities of water in your eyes

MI DIOS NO LLEGA   MI DIOS NO VIENE
MI DIOS NO VUELVE

Empapado   chorreante de agua   el Estadio Nacional iba
emergiendo en la resaca

Con la voz de *Los Prisioneros* cantando "Por qué no se van
del país" y chicos amarrados en los camarines   con las
manos en la nuca   coreando de lejos esas canciones

Mientras el amanecer se alzaba mostrando las graderías y
en el fondo la cancha de fútbol entera cubierta de mar y
era como un cielo de púas las olas   blancas cubriendo de
espumas los roqueríos

Cuando arrojados desde los estadios chilenos alcanzamos
a ver los roqueríos y luego el vacío infinito del mar Es
que los chicos nunca regresaron: tocan *Los Prisioneros*
y es el dios que no regresa   el dios que no viene   el dios
que no vuelve soplándonos como sopla el alba muerta
como sopla el amor muerto   como sopla la mañana
muerta frente a los despojos todavía azules de la noche

MY GOD DOESN'T ARRIVE   MY GOD ISN'T COMING
MY GOD DOESN'T RETURN

Soaked   drenched in water   the Estadio Nacional went
on emerging from the undertow

With the voice of *Los Prisioneros* singing "Why don't they
leave our country" and kids tied up in dressing rooms
hands at their necks   shouting out from far off those songs

As dawn rose up revealing the stands and beneath the whole
soccer field covered over by the sea and it was like a sky of
barbs the waves   white   covering with foam the
rocky shore

When we were thrown down from the Chilean stadiums
we managed to see the rocks and then the vacant end-
lessness of the sea   It's just that the kids never came back:
they play *Los Prisioneros* and it's the god that doesn't make it
the god that doesn't come   the god that doesn't return
blowing us like it blows the dead daybreak like the dead love
like the dead morning blows before still blue remains of night

MI DIOS NO LLORA MI DIOS NO SANGRA
MI DIOS NO SIENTE

My God is a little boy   My God is a fat man   escribían
los bombarderos en el cielo 060845

Atravesando el inclinado horizonte   las nubes que se iban
quedando abajo   las islas reflejándose en el mar negro de
las alturas

Donde las cañoneadas escuadras giran a la deriva como si
emprendieran un largo regreso y era una imagen de sueño
el color negro pizarra del Pacífico recortándose al fondo
frente al sol que nacía

En el cielo 060845   y eran millones y millones de edades
millones de amaneceres   millones de planetas naciendo
allí donde nos vimos flotar con los brazos caídos como
flotan los ahogados mirando abajo las cumbres nevadas
*Mi dios es un niño pequeño   Mi dios es un hombre
gordo* seguían escribiendo los bombarderos sobre el
cielo mientras el nuevo sol subía y no eran espejismos
las ciudades de cenizas naciendo en la calcinada aurora

MY GOD DOESN'T WEEP   MY GOD DOESN'T BLEED
MY GOD DOESN'T FEEL

My God is a little boy   My God is a fat man   the bombers
would write in sky 060845

Traversing the sloped horizon   the clouds that continued
further below   the islands mirrored in the black sea of
the heights

Where the bomb squads twirl adrift as if they set out on
a long return and it was an image of dreams the black
chalkboard color Pacific gashing down below before
the aborning sun

In sky 060845   and they were millions and millions of
ages millions of dawns   millions of planets being born
there where we saw ourselves float with fallen arms
like the drowned float looking down the snow-fallen
peaks   *My god is a little boy   My god is a fat*
man the bombers went on writing over the sky
as the new sun rose and they were not mirages
those ashen cities being born in the charred aurora

MI DIOS NO MIRA   MI DIOS NO OYE
MI DIOS NO ES

Mi dios no mira   Mi dios no oye   Mi dios no es   y eran
aviones en fuga escribiendo en el cielo

Sobrevolando las irradiadas ciudades que iban subiendo
en la inmensidad del alba como lejanos sueños olvidados
al despertar

Y son como brumosos prados que reaparecen en un sueño
o colinas reaparecidas de pronto   imágenes con jardines
y niños que juegan a volverse cenizas bajo las abrasadas
ciudades

Mientras los bombarderos del sueño y la locura vuelan
sobre ellas escribiendo en el cielo   *Mi dios ¿por qué?*
Dios mío ¿no me oyes?   Amor mío ¿no me ves? Y es
la piel pavorosamente quemada de un niño el cielo
pavorosamente quemado del amanecer . . .   Se reporta:
miles de niños suben como pequeños soles al amanecer
Se reporta el hongo del amanecer   Se reportan mares
de ceniza y sangre bajo los cielos en fuga del amanecer

MY GOD DOESN'T LOOK   MY GOD DOESN'T HEAR
MY GOD IS NOT

My god doesn't look   My god doesn't hear   My god is not   and
they were planes fleeing writing in the sky

Soaring over the radiated cities that went on rising in the
enormousness of sunrise like distant dreams forgotten
in their wake

And they're like hazed meadows that appear again in a dream
or hills that suddenly appear again   images with gardens
and kids that play just to become ashes again below the
blazed cities

While the bombers of the dream and madness soar over them
writing in the sky   *My god is Why?   My god is Don't you hear
me?   My love Don't you see me?* And the sky is the terrifyingly
scorched skin of a child terrifyingly burned by dawn . . .
They report: thousands of children rise like small suns at
dawn   They report the mushroom at dawn   They report
oceans of ashes and blood below the fleeing skies of dawn

¿ERAS TÚ PAPÁ?

Después de cinco días esperando que se despejara
la neblina sobre la costa norte pude ver los
acantilados. Kilómetros y kilómetros de paredes
de granito cortándose a pique y mil metros más
abajo el Pacífico. Había imaginado unas
frases escritas sobre esos murallones, veintidós
exactamente, de amor, de locura y de muerte
recortándose sobre ellos. Me las imaginé en un
sueño. La llanura del desierto de Atacama que se
interrumpía de golpe, luego el abismo y al
fondo el mar. Años después morí. Eran millones
y millones de hombres y mujeres arrojándose,
muchedumbres inacabables que se detenían por
un instante en el borde de los paredones y luego
se lanzaban. Algunos lo hacían tomados de la
mano, se miraban a los ojos y daban el último
paso, otros sostenían niños en sus brazos y
lloraban quedamente mientras el viento del
desierto hacía flamear sus ropas. Sentí un brazo
posarse en mi hombro ¿eras tú papá? y el vacío
se abrió bajo mis pies sin estruendo, igual que
una boca muda y dulce. Al frente, el azul del
inmenso amanecer se iba fundiendo con el
Pacífico y las frases de amor, de locura y de
muerte, se me pegaron en los labios también sin
estruendo, suavemente, como un último silencio.

Así:

WAS IT YOU PAPA?

After five days of waiting for the fog to clear
over the northern coast I could see the cliffs.
Kilometers upon kilometers of jagging granite
walls and a thousand meters below, the Pacific.
I had imagined lines written upon those massive
walls, exactly twenty-two of love, of madness
and death incising into them. I imagined them
in a dream. The plain of the desert of Atacama
suddenly interrupted, then the abyss and then
to the bottom of the sea. I died years later. They
were millions upon millions of women and men
throwing themselves, interminable crowds of
people that held back for a moment at the edge
of the vast walls and then cast themselves down.
Some did it holding hands, they looked into
one another's eyes and took the last step, others
held children in their arms and cried steadily
while the desert wind flailed their clothes about.
I felt an arm rest on my shoulder. Was it you
papa? And the emptiness opened beneath my
feet without a sound, just like a sweet mute
mouth. Before me, the blue of the immense
sunrise merged with the Pacific and the lines of
love, of madness and death, stuck to my lips also
without a sound, softly, like an irrevocable silence.

Like this:

EL ÚLTIMO PROYECTO

22 frases proyectadas sobre los acantilados
Sólo se verán desde el mar

VERÁS UN MAR DE PIEDRAS
VERÁS MARGARITAS EN EL MAR
VERÁS UN DIOS DE HAMBRE
VERÁS EL HAMBRE
VERÁS UN PAÍS DE SED
VERÁS CUMBRES
VERÁS EL MAR EN LAS CUMBRES
VERÁS ESFUMADOS RÍOS
VERÁS AMORES EN FUGA
VERÁS MONTAÑAS EN FUGA
VERÁS IMBORRABLES ERRATAS
VERÁS EL ALBA
VERÁS SOLDADOS EN EL ALBA
VERÁS AURORAS COMO SANGRE
VERÁS BORRADAS FLORES
VERÁS FLOTAS ALEJÁNDOSE
VERÁS LAS NIEVES DEL FIN
VERÁS CIUDADES DE AGUA
VERÁS CIELOS EN FUGA
VERÁS UN PARAÍSO VACÍO
VERÁS QUE SE VA
VERÁS NO VER
Y LLORARÁS

THE LAST PROJECT

22 lines projected onto the cliffs
Visible only from the sea

YOU'LL SEE A SEA OF STONES
YOU'LL SEE DAISIES IN THE SEA
YOU'LL SEE A GOD OF HUNGER
YOU'LL SEE HUNGER
YOU'LL SEE A COUNTRY OF THIRST
YOU'LL SEE PEAKS
YOU'LL SEE THE SEA IN THE PEAKS
YOU'LL SEE VANISHING RIVERS
YOU'LL SEE LOVES FLEEING
YOU'LL SEE MOUNTAINS FLEEING
YOU'LL SEE INDELIBLE MISPRINTS
YOU'LL SEE DAWN
YOU'LL SEE SOLDIERS AT DAWN
YOU'LL SEE AURORAS LIKE BLOOD
YOU'LL SEE FLOWERS ERASED
YOU'LL SEE FLEETS WITHDRAW
YOU'LL SEE SNOWS OF THE END
YOU'LL SEE CITIES OF WATER
YOU'LL SEE SKIES FLEEING
YOU'LL SEE AN EMPTY PARADISE
YOU'LL SEE IT LEAVE
YOU'LL SEE NOT SEEING
AND YOU WILL WEEP

VERÁS AURORAS COMO SANGRE

VERÁS BORRADAS FLORES

VERÁS CIELOS EN FUGA

VERÁS QUE SE VA

VERÁS NO VER

Y LLORARÁS

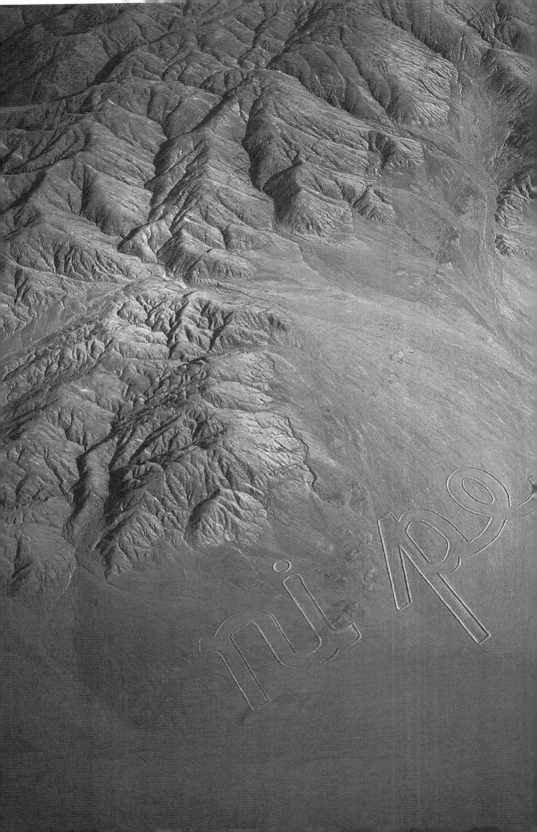

no pain no fear

WORKS BY RAÚL ZURITA

Early Publications

"El sermón de la montaña." In *Quijada*. Valparaíso: Ediciones Universidad Técnica Federico Santa María, 1971.

"La tiempo blanca para nuestro mundo negro." In *Nueva poesía chilena*, ed. Martín Micharvegas. Buenos Aires: Editorial Noé, 1972.

"Allá lejos." In *Chilkatún*. Valparaíso: Instituto Chileno–Francés de Cultura, 1973.

"Áreas verdes." In *Manuscritos*. Santiago: Departamento de Estudios Humanísticos, Universidad de Chile, 1975.

"¿Qué es el paraíso?" In *CAL 3*, Santiago de Chile, 1979.

Poetry (FIRST EDITIONS)

Purgatorio. Santiago: Editorial Universitaria, 1979.

Anteparaíso. Santiago: Editores Asociados, 1982.

El paraíso está vacío. Santiago: 1984.

Canto a su amor desaparecido. Santiago: Editorial Universitaria, 1985.

El amor de Chile. Santiago: Montt & Palumbo, 1987.

La vida nueva. Santiago: Editorial Universitaria, 1994.

Canto de los ríos que se aman. Santiago: Editorial Universitaria, 1995.

El día más blanco. Santiago: Anagrama, 2000.

Poemas militantes. Santiago: Dolmen Ediciones, 2000.

INRI. Madrid: Editorial Visor, 2004.

Mi mejilla es el cielo estrellado. Mexico City: Ediciones Aldus, 2004

Tu vida derrumbándose. Buenos Aires: Eloisa cartonera, 2005.

Los países muertos. Santiago: Ediciones Tácitas, Santiago de Chile, 2006.

LVN/El país de tablas. Mexico City: Ediciones Monte Carmelo, 2006.

Mis amigos creen. Casa de Poesía, San José de Costa Rica, 2006.

Cinco fragmentos. Santiago: Animita Cartonera, 2007.

In Memoriam. Santiago: Ediciones Tácitas, 2007.

Las ciudades de agua. Mexico City: Ediciones ERA, 2007.

Cuadernos de guerra. Santiago: Ediciones Tácitas, 2010.

Zurita. Santiago: Ediciones Universidad Diego Portales, 2011.

El sermón de la montaña. Santiago: Editorial Cuneta, 2012.

Tu vida rompiéndose, Santiago and Barcelona: Editorial Lumen, 2015.

Prose

Literatura, lenguaje y sociedad en Chile, 1973–1983. Santiago: Ediciones Céneca, 1983.

Sobre el amor, el sufrimiento y el nuevo milenio. Santiago: Editorial Andrés Bello, 2000.

Cantares: 42 nuevas voces de la poesía chilena. Santiago: Editorial LOM, 2004.

El río de la poesía chilena. New Delhi: Center for Spanish Studies, University of New Delhi, 2004.

Los poemas muertos. Mexico City: Ediciones Libros del Umbral, 2006.

Saber morir: Conversaciones (with Ilan Stavans). Santiago: Universidad Diego Portales, 2014.

LIST OF POEMS

De *PURGATORIO* | From *PURGATORY*

mis amigos creen | *my friends think*   4

EN EL MEDIO DEL CAMINO | IN THE MIDDLE OF
THE ROAD

    EGO SUM QUI SUM   8

    Me llamo Raquel | *My name is Rachel*   9

    XXII   12

    LXIII   14

DESIERTOS | DESERTS

    COMO UN SUEÑO | LIKE A DREAM   18

    QUIÉN PODRÍA LA ENORME DIGNIDAD DEL
    DESIERTO | WHO COULD THE ENORMOUS
    DIGNITY OF THE DESERT   20

    I. A LAS INMACULADAS LLANURAS | I. TO THE
    IMMACULATE PLAINS   22

    EL DESIERTO DE ATACAMA II | THE DESERT
    OF ATACAMA II   24

    EL DESIERTO DE ATACAMA III | THE DESERT
    OF ATACAMA III   26

    VII. EL DESIERTO DE ATACAMA | VII. THE
    DESERT OF ATACAMA   28

ÁREAS VERDES | GREEN AREAS

    Han visto extenderse estos pastos infinitos? |
    Have you seen these infinite pastures extend themselves?   32

    Comprended las fúnebres manchas de la vaca |
    Comprehend the cow's woeful stains   34

    Quién daría por esas auras manchadas? | *Who would*
    give for those stained auras?   36

MI AMOR DE DIOS | MY LOVE OF GOD

    LOS CAMPOS DEL HAMBRE | THE FIELDS OF
    HUNGER   40

    LAS LLANURAS DEL DOLOR | THE PLAINS OF
    PAIN   42

    MI AMOR DE DIOS | MY LOVE OF GOD   44

LA VIDA NUEVA | NEW LIFE

PARADISO | PARADISO   48

DE *ANTEPARAÍSO* | FROM *ANTEPARADISE*

LA VIDA NUEVA | NEW LIFE   52

LAS UTOPÍAS | UTOPIAS

    LAS PLAYAS DE CHILE I | THE BEACHES OF
    CHILE I   62

    LAS PLAYAS DE CHILE VII | THE BEACHES OF
    CHILE VII   64

    LAS PLAYAS DE CHILE X | THE BEACHES OF
    CHILE X   66

CORDILLERAS | CORDILLERAS

    /CI/   70

    /CII/   72

/CIII/   74

PASTORAL | PASTORAL

     PASTORAL | PASTORAL   78

     EL GRITO DE MARÍA | MARIA'S SCREAM   80

     TODO HA SIDO CONSUMADO | ALL HAS BEEN
     CONSUMED   82

     II   84

     X   86

     IDILIO GENERAL | COMMON IDYLL   88

     ESPLENDOR EN EL VIENTO | SPLENDOR IN
     THE WIND   90

CANTO A SU AMOR DESAPARECIDO | SONG FOR HIS
     DISAPPEARED LOVE   92

DE LA VIDA NUEVA | FROM NEW LIFE

LA VIDA NUEVA | NEW LIFE

     LA VIDA NUEVA | NEW LIFE   134

I. LOS RÍOS ARROJADOS | I. THE RIVERS CAST DOWN

     LA SÉPTIMA | THE SEVENTH   138

     LOS RÍOS ARROJADOS | THE RIVERS CAST DOWN   140

     EL PRIMER PACÍFICO | THE FIRST PACIFIC   142

     CANTO DE LOS RÍOS QUE SE AMAN | SONG OF
     THE RIVERS THAT LOVE ONE ANOTHER   144

     HÉCTOR GESSEL PADRE LARGA EL SEGUNDO
     CANTO DE LOS RÍOS | HECTOR GESSEL FATHER
     BEGINS THE SECOND SONG OF THE RIVERS   146

II. LAS BORRADAS ESTRELLAS | II. THE STARS ERASED

    JOSEFINA PESSOLO ROMPE A LLORAR FRENTE
    A SU NIETO | JOSEFINA PESSOLO STARTS TO
    WEEP IN FRONT OF HER GRANDSON   150

III. LOS RÍOS DEL CIELO | III. THE RIVERS OF SKY

    EL PACÍFICO ES EL CIELO | THE PACIFIC IS
    THE SKY   154

    EL CRUCE DE LOS CONTINENTES | THE
    CROSSING OF CONTINENTS   156

    LOS DESAPARECIDOS LEVANTAN SUS CARAS
    DESDE LOS DESIERTOS | THE DISAPPEARED
    LIFT UP THEIR FACES FROM THE DESERTS   158

DE *POEMAS MILITANTES* | FROM *MILITANT POEMS*

    CANTO I | SONG I   162

    CANTO XI | SONG XI   164

DE *INRI* | FROM *INRI*

EL MAR | THE SEA

    Sorprendentes carnadas | *Strange flesh*   170

    Se oyen días enteros hundiéndose | *You can hear whole
    days sinking*   172

    Oí un cielo y un mar alucinantes | *I heard a deranged
    sky and sea*   174

BRUNO SE DOBLA, CAE | BRUNO BENDS OVER, FALLS

    Al frente las montañas emergen | *In the foreground the
    mountains emerge*   178

    Las ciudades pequeñas son blancas | *At night the small
    cities are white*   180

La tierra que cubre a Bruno es negra | The dirt that
covers Bruno is black   182

Recuerdo un pasaje del mar | I recall a path along the sea   184

Bruno está muerto | Bruno's dead   186

Se dobla, cae | He bends over, falls   188

EL DESCENSO | THE DESCENT   190

DE ZURITA | FROM ZURITA

TU ROTA TARDE | YOUR BROKEN AFTERNOON

    CIELO ABAJO | SKY BELOW   196

    CIELO ABAJO | SKY BELOW   198

    CIELO ABAJO | SKY BELOW   200

    1973   202

    IN MEMORIAM: CON OTRO ATARDECER | IN
    MEMORIAM: WITH ANOTHER DUSK   204

    MI NOMBRE: AKIRA KUROSAWA | MY NAME:
    AKIRA KUROSAWA   206

    MARGARITAS EN EL MAR | DAISIES IN THE SEA   208

    SUEÑO 210 / A KUROSAWA | DREAM 211 / FOR
    KUROSAWA   210

    SUEÑO 212 / A KUROSAWA | DREAM 213 / FOR
    KUROSAWA   212

    SUEÑO 214 / A KUROSAWA | DREAM 215 / FOR
    KUROSAWA   214

TU ROTA NOCHE | YOUR BROKEN NIGHT

    ¿DESPERTAREMOS ENTONCES? | THEN WILL
    WE WAKE?   218

    PRISIÓN ESTADIO CHILE | ESTADIO CHILE PRISON   220

PRISIÓN GRILLA GRIMALDI | VILLA GRIMALDI
PRISON   222

Y AÚN NO AMANECE | AND STILL NO DAWN   224

TU ROTO AMANECER | YOUR BROKEN DAWN

AUSCHWITZ   228

AUSCHWITZ   230

AUSCHWITZ   232

PAULINA WENDT   234

PAULINA WENDT   236

PAULINA WENDT   238

MI DIOS NO LLEGA   MI DIOS NO VIENE   MI
DIOS NO VUELVE | MY GOD DOESN'T ARRIVE
MY GOD ISN'T COMING   MY GOD DOESN'T
RETURN   240

MI DIOS NO LLORA   MI DIOS NO SANGRA   MI
DIOS NO SIENTE | MY GOD DOESN'T WEEP
MY GOD DOESN'T BLEED   MY GOD DOESN'T
FEEL   242

MI DIOS NO MIRA   MI DIOS NO OYE   MI DIOS
NO ES | MY GOD DOESN'T LOOK   MY GOD
DOESN'T HEAR   MY GOD IS NOT   244

¿ERAS TÚ PAPA? | WAS IT YOU PAPA?   246

EL ÚLTIMO PROYECTO | THE LAST PROJECT   248

ni pena ni miedo | no pain no fear   256

ILLUSTRATION CREDITS

The cover photograph was taken by Anna Deeny Morales in the Desert of Atacama.

From *Anteparadise*, the photographs of "MI DIOS ES" skywriting over Queens, New York, were taken by Ana María López Sotomayor.

From *Zurita*, the cliff photographs were taken by Nicolás Piwonka.

The photograph of the "ni pena ni miedo" geoglyph in the Desert of Atacama was taken by the Chilean Air Force.

Book design and typesetting by Marianne Jankowski

Composed in Adobe Font Folio's Electra LT Std. and Atlas Font Foundry's Novel San Hair 18

Printed on 70# Finch Offset and bound by Sheridan Books